TEEN THEATER

A GUIDE TO PLAY PRODUCTION AND

NEW YORK   TORONTO   LONDON

Teen

SIX ROYALTY-FREE PLAYS

Theater

by EDWIN and NATHALIE GROSS

foreword by MARGARET C. SCOGGIN

with line drawings by EDWIN GROSS

McGRAW-HILL BOOK COMPANY

To

MERRILY

for future reference

CONTENTS

FOREWORD

THERE is magic in the theater. At some time in his life almost everyone wants to act in or "put on" a play. I know, because libraries are besieged by persons who ask about play selection or staging or costuming or directing or acting. There are many good technical handbooks on all aspects of play production; however, there are all too few which put just the right amount of help into one simple and eminently readable guide.

Teen Theater is what most beginners are looking for. It is timely, specific, and well organized. Without presupposing an experienced coach or leader around the corner, it gives all the necessary information for any amateur group who want to know exactly how to set up plays. From the very first chapter on organization which explains the division of responsibilities to the last which is a Glossary of Theater Terms, this really anticipates all problems and questions. It does it, too, without oversimplifying and without sacrificing the professional's interest in smoothness and finish. In short, it is a book to read, use, and assimilate. In addition to giving step-by-step aid in production, the authors have included six modern plays for teen-age actors, complete with staging and acting tips.

And now a word to club leaders and teachers! Often a club wants to give a play or an English teacher is handed the extra assignment of dramatics coach. Don't let such an event disturb you. *Teen Theater* will lead you and your group to pleasurable and profitable play production.

Margaret C. Scoggin

Letter of Introduction

Dear Teen Theater-winger:

HERE is a Guide to Play Production for you that accents the simple-practical.

The Guide escorts you around the theater—on stage, backstage, and out front—from "Let's do" to "All through." It applies to every kind of play, long and short, comic and serious, modern and classical, easy and difficult. If you are a novice at working in the theater, it will pilot you. If you have done plays before, it will refresh you on the assorted parts that make the whole. For ready reference, too, there is a Glossary.

To spur you into production, we have included six one-act comedies about genial teen-agers. They have it's-happening-today situations and familiar settings. We hope you will relish them in reading—and do them with a group.

Before you carry on, though, give ear to some fundamentals.

HELP WANTED—EXPERIENCE NOT NECESSARY! That's right! To put on a play the only "must" is a core of interested persons. Maybe you are already a member of the Make-Up Box, Mask and Wig, Green Room, Thespian, or plain old Drama Society. Maybe at your school, church, camp, grange, or "rec" center there is a players' group you can join. Maybe one of your clubs wants to tackle a play. No chance there? Recruit some friends and dig in. Informally as that, many a flourishing amateur company got under way.

Do not forget that you can put on a show anywhere, under most any conditions. That is because the theater is intriguingly flexible. It can bask in widely varying shades of realism and make-believe. You have immense latitude on talent, time, money, ideas, and ambition.

Financing a production should not ever stymie you. A parent institution may back you. And then there are ways to bring money in—and to hold expenses down. As our Guide states, again and again, drama can thrive on a wispy wallet—plus ingenuity.

No need to linger on where to find your audiences. You have friends, schoolmates, admiring family. You can also take steps to draw some of the great general public that is always seeking entertainment. For ways how, check the section on Publicity.

Some reminders: a one-act play is often given along with a party, dance, meeting, assembly, festival—to magnify the occasion. Many ambitious teen troupes have done guest showings at hospitals, settlement houses, service camps, schools, play tournaments.

You can conveniently build a bill of one-acts into a major theater event. To spread work, fun, and cost, have a different group do each play. Incidentally, this book's *Dooley and the Amateur Hour* has a peculiar merit. It is expandable—by specialty numbers—to any length *you* desire.

Suggestions for spending the profits you are likely to make: donate to charities; support a school band or paper; splurge on class gifts, a club trip, team uniforms; send a delegate to a convention. Or let some charity begin at home and build up your "nut" for future shows.

And now for the brass ring on the merry-go-round! It is fashionable to make florid claims for everything from flea powder to soft water. But it is safe to *guarantee* your *personal* profit from amateur dramatics. That is edging out on a limb, but the tree is certainly mighty sturdy.

Right up front is the delightful fact you will have fun. It is heady, exhilarating, to be part of a show. Any part. In it, or around it. Broadway's Mary Martin says, "My happiest period was probably that in high school when I was . . . in our school plays back home."

You will also be picking up poise, skill, and confidence. And learning about working with people, and meeting the public.

Self-expression is another satisfaction. Not the show-offy kind —but the sense of helping a creative team effort with your talents. There is elbow room for such wide variety: directing, acting, designing, painting, costuming, carpentry, make-up, lighting, publicity, business managing. Truly, the list is endless. Name your bent; the theater—most encompassing of all arts—can use it.

Too, you will be fostering a hobby immune to changes in vogue—and so versatile in service. Move to a new school or community and you will quickly feel at home if you join a little theater. At a vacation spot, help with dramatics and you are with friends. At school, drama is usually a stimulating and glamorous extracurricular activity. Best of all, the pastime can grow with you. Bulging waistline, doddery step—these are no hindrance if you are adept at dyeing a costume, directing a cast or crew, facing the footlights.

Have you noticed that when you learn a new name or word it seems to crop up everywhere? Well, play production begets so many "new's" that horizons stre-etch. Insight into people (counting parents, friends, and yourself) is deepened. Ditto appreciation of speech, movement, the look of persons, places, and things. In any audience—even at a football rally or an auction—a grasp of showmanship widens your pleasure.

Perhaps you aspire to forge your future in the professional entertainment world via stage, TV, radio, movies. If so, to you an aside: amateur dramatics is *superb* grounding. You gain a solid concept of all that goes into a production. You test and train your talent in front of "live" audiences, unmatched teachers as any top-runger will tell you. Before battling against the no-holds-barred competition, you will have given cagey thought to the query, "Is this *really* for me?"

If you're not an old-timer at reading plays, some urge-you-on's: you can cover loads more stage fare in an armchair than in a theater. Plays in print are tremendously satisfying. Long on dialogue and short on description, they move swiftly with what HE said, and what SHE said, what HE said next, and what SHE did about it. Much of the world's most enriching literature—from Aeschylus to this year's Pulitzer Prize winner—is in dramatic form.

About the plays in this book: *Belle, Date-Time,* and *Dooley and the Amateur Hour* have appeared in the magazine *Seventeen* and have been cited in Margaret Mayorga's *Best One-Act Plays* series. *Marko Goes a Courtin'* has won a national award. And *She Loves Him Yes* and *A Party Is Born* have been produced with thumping success by teen groups.

Now pitch in—with zest and imagination. Harness substitutes, short cuts, and do-withouts to suit *your* purse and purpose. Have fun—and the best of luck to you!

Yours for lifelong pleasure
with plays,
Edwin and Nathalie Gross

Guide to Play Production

ORGANIZATION

ONE person's will to do a play can spark a production. But the surest way to achieve smooth performances is to *assign responsibility*. Maybe you will be doubling up, but decide who is supposed to do what!

Here is a suggested pattern of organization.

1) In amateur theater the *director* is usually the captain. He (can be a *she* just as well, of course, and that holds for every post) is responsible for the over-all show. The director casts the actors, plans stage action and line delivery, conducts rehearsals. Backstage and frequently business staffers refer final decisions to him. Though his coworkers may be skillful enough to deserve loose reins, he must blend their abilities. He does not have to be an expert. Far from it. But by and large it is his interpretation of a script that is mounted.

The director may also act and fill other offices.

2) The *actors* are those hardworking people who have the pleasure of repeatedly knocking themselves out before an audience to woo approval. They are immediately responsible to the director. They contribute most when teamwork (not self-trumpeting!) dominates their trouping.

3) The *scene designer*—at times termed "technical director," "technician" or "production manager"—is a jack-of-trades. He is responsible to the director. He conceives the stage set, the physical means showing where and when a play takes place, and he oversees the execution. Scenic effects—costumes, lighting, furnishings, and "props"—fall under his wing. Helps if he has a knack for décor, carpentry, and directing a crew, if he is lucky enough to have one!

4) The *stage manager* works with both the cast and backstage staff. In a sense he is traffic cop. He does not build scenery but knows where it has to go. He does not act but is familiar with every detail of the play. Of course, he can act and build if he wants to or is needed.

As coordinator of the stagecraft end, the stage manager checks that the following have executed their missions:

5) The *property man*, who sees that props required by the script are assembled.

6) The *costume head*, who collects or makes costumes and confirms they are in good repair for each performance. (This post can be omitted for the easy-to-dress plays in this book.)

7) The *make-up man*, who supervises make-up.

8) The *light man*, who arranges lights where they are needed and operates them on cue.

9) The *sound* or *special-effects man*, who produces his effects on cue. (This post is often not needed.)

The stage manager frequently doubles as *prompter, call boy,* or any of the above. He keeps the prompt book at rehearsals, pulls or signals for the drawing of the curtain, and governs shifting of the scenery. Also, as the director's lieutenant, he may even help out by handling rehearsals. By playtime he is so "up" on lines that he is sometimes corralled as understudy if one is needed.

10) The *publicity man* figures out where his audience lies. Then he plans the best use of newspaper stories, posters, ads, assembly announcements, TV and radio spots, and other devices to attract it. The more "tom-tomming" he can get for *free,* the better.

11) The *business manager* handles finances. His is a vital job, especially if, as is often practical, he does publicity and is *house manager.* He is Mr. Budget to the director, knowing soberly how much can be spent. He devises means of raising money, pays bills, decides on the price of tickets and has them printed, sets fees for program advertising, keeps record of the entrance and exit of cold cash. He may have assistants for ticket sales, program editing, and house management. This last means assigning ushers and looking after audience comfort.

If your group is small, remember that you can triple and quadruple assignments. A core of keen people can see a production through, covering all acting, off-stage, and business phases.

When you have more willing workers than titles, appoint committees to various jobs. Having a finger in a production is satisfying and self-expressing. Make room for all who want to contribute!

DIRECTING

THE director is Big Chief of a production. His alchemy (a polite name for *work*) molds the acting, scenery, lights, and costumes into an effective whole. And as a specific job, he runs rehearsals.

Where is this key man found? The answer is apparent . . . in every dramatic group. Every director has to have a first try. If a theater-wise person is not around, most eligible is a theater-bitten. The more a director has a yen for plays—takes part in, sees, and reads them—the better his chances of doing a rewarding show. Since he handles people, though, he needs streaks of tact and humor.

When you take on the assignment of director, you realize you must compromise between what you would *like* to do and what your means allow. Few absolutes exist in the theater. After all, even a stage itself is dispensable. Plays are given every day in parts of rooms and outdoor clearings. During the Middle Ages troupes acted on wagons!

Matter of fact, limited resources can stimulate imagination. There is an old saying: "Starve a director and you'll get better work from him."

Make your plans after reviewing your play, personnel, budget, and equipment. Obviously you must delegate authority in technical matters. Visualize the set—and swap ideas with the scene designer (if you have one). See that work begins on the mechanics of production. Check with crew heads from time to time and be available for consultation. The stage manager can serve to a great extent as your go-between, leaving you free to concentrate on rehearsals.

It is very wise to draw up a rehearsal calendar. Estimate roughly how much will be covered at each meeting, how many will be needed in all. This will help you avoid the common error of over-rehearsing the start of a play and neglecting the middle and end.

To sidestep actors' gripes and stalls, announce your time table at tryouts. Then you can cast only those who promise to be faithful. You are likely to be confronted with unavoidable delays, but do discourage frivolous absences.

As you first read your play you may find you have fairly well decided whom you would like to cast in each role. Still, conduct tryouts with an open mind. The person who most looks the part often is not the one who can breathe the most life into it on stage.

Before holding tryouts, make your play available to would-be actors. Also, at tryouts give a brief explanation of the story and the roles.

For tryouts have two or three candidates read a scene of your play aloud together—or a few scenes. Note that "scene," in this sense, covers a single episode. It will probably begin and end with an actor's entrance or exit, or a sharp change in mood. Select scenes with dramatic speeches so you can judge ability to project emotion. And preferably, get your actors up on a stage or in front of the room.

You may have to call candidates back to read for you a few times before you can announce your cast. Continue to be impartial. Who is handicapped if you choose the most popular instead of the most talented? You. Your work is rated in large measure through the actors.

When you are short-handed, actors can play more than one part. *Belle, Dooley and the Amateur Hour* and *A Party Is Born,* for example, lend themselves well to doubling. Stage custom traditionally programs a doubler once as himself, then with the surname "Spelvin"—usually "George" or "Georgette." But there is nothing against giving credit where it is due. It is probably more sensible!

If you do not have enough males, cast more girls. Pick larger ones, and those with voices of lower range, as your men. All-male groups often recruit boys for female roles with reverse considerations of size and voice.

You can lay important groundwork before the first rehearsal.

Read your play most carefully. As prime interpreter of the playwright's ideas, think over setting, mood, characters, and dialogue. Find the "big scenes" and "plot lines" (those speeches telling the story) that you will want to emphasize. Decide which scenes can be played more relaxedly, perhaps in the more remote left, right, and upper portions of your stage. Make any changes in the text that may be strategic because a reference has become dated, or is not suitable for your audience.

Then "block out" the action. This means foresee, as far as convenient at this time, placements of the actors, major bits of "business" and movements, standings and sittings, entrances and exits. Many plays include fairly full stage directions. To the degree your script lacks them, see with your mind's eye and fill in.

Some painstaking directors aid their imaginations by maneuvering toy figures or buttons on a sketch of the ground plan or on a model stage. Method here is purely a personal matter. Incidentally, you will find a ground plan with each of this book's plays.

Do your blocking scene by scene. Bear in mind that you want your actors to tell the story, set the locale and atmosphere, and portray character. Also, as George Kelly said in his famous satire on little theater, *The Torch-Bearers,* you direct traffic. You have to "tell the players where to go on the stage, so they won't be running into each other."

Too, sense the amount of movement each scene needs to keep it from becoming dull—and to keep the picture the actors make on stage relatively in balance—and to keep the pace true. Do not feel that you have to make movement incessant. Use memories of plays you have seen as reference. Also use your knowledge of how people behave.

In general, movement on stage, especially in a realistic or

naturalistic play, should appear to have some reason for happening. For example, an actor might cross the stage to pick up a magazine, to talk to someone, to straighten a picture frame, to find an ash tray. Whatever your setting, it is loaded with likely "motivations." The move can come before, during, or after delivery of a line. Often watching your actors will show you what is effective.

Try to use all areas of your stage at some time without resorting to one section too monotonously. Variety helps to create naturalness and sustain interest and excitement. If other factors—like color, level, and mass—are about equal, downstage is more attention-arresting than upstage. And action at center is more dominant than at right or left.

When you want two actors to "share" a scene equally, keep them somewhat oppositely placed and equally visible to the audience. When one character is to be "given" the scene, station him more or less upstage of the other. Then the less important character will have to turn toward him and will not reveal as much of his face to the audience.

Plays generally have a pattern of rising action or "dramatic build." Like a close ball game's, their suspense grows and grows. As your climax approaches, aim to convey this increased tension. You will usually find it strategic to (a) bring action center stage, (b) see that actors are grouped so focus falls on characters in conflict, (c) step up volume and tempo. The writing in most plays helps you achieve this effect. Often there is a brief interlude of falling action, commonly called a "drop scene," before the final curtain.

There are directors, by the way, who prefer to do almost all their blocking at rehearsals. In most cases this system is *not* recommended. It puts a strain on the actors, and sessions tend to bog down with too many suggestions. On the other hand, you can expect many revisions to crop up during rehearsals from your own observations and from actor contributions.

Let us assume, then, that you have come to grips with your play—and written down some plans. Now you can call first rehearsal fortified by more than a vague idea of what you want and how to get it.

At the first rehearsal everybody usually sits. And the actors read the play aloud. Arrived at are a common understanding of the drama and each player's role. Here is the time to catch errors in the typing of parts.

Incidentally, director and stage manager need complete play scripts. When you cannot buy all the copies you would like, and do not have access to a mimeograph or ditto machine, you might decide to save typing by having some of your actors work from "sides." Sides—which are frequently used in the professional theater—contain only the particular actor's cues of a few words and then his stage directions and dialogue. This is how GEORGE's sides for *Date-Time* would begin:

- - - - - Come in here, George.
    [*You enter U.R.C. with Alice.*]
    [*Well-poised, genially*]
Good evening, everybody. How's the Mygatt family tonight?

- - - - - Good evening, George.
Hello there, Mrs. Mygatt. How have you been?

- - - - - Just fine.
You're looking mighty well this evening.

- - - - - some tie, George!
    [*Pleasantly*]
So you like knitted ones, too?
    [*Loud whisper*]
I'll tell you a secret, Bill. They're my weakness!

Your actors will grasp their parts more thoroughly, though, if they have the entire play. Provide them with it if you can.

You will find most casts learn best by working on a play piecemeal, mastering one scene at a time. At early rehearsals some directors like to mount the stage themselves and suggest to the actors movements and inflections that are in character. Others try to lead the players to arrive at their own suitable interpretations. Whatever the way, each actor must become sure of when, where, and how he sits, stands, and moves—and of the delivery of all his lines! As action and business grow definitive, the director, actors, and stage manager should record them in their scripts.

Whenever you rehearse, create a set. If you are not using your stage, chalk off an acting area on the floor. Make the dimensions of this ground plan conform to the stage you will give your performance on. Indicate all your entrances.

Until you have furniture, chalk its dimensions, too. Then you can work out the action in detail. However, try to use your stage and replace chalk with furniture as early as possible. Actors will learn faster and feel more at home come opening night.

From the beginning have players use hand props—items they handle in the play like dishes, telephone, brief case, pipe, eyeglasses. Work with substitutes till you have the real ones.

Encourage learning parts quickly: movements as well as lines. Suggestion: outlaw scripts at a definite date. Be firm. Anyone who has not memorized by deadline just fumbles along—with the aid of a prompter, of course.

At later rehearsals keep an eye on how well you are achieving the over-all directoral design. You have to rely on your own instinct in great degree to tell you when the pace of a scene is just right, when the actors are delivering their lines most effectively. Once in a while it helps to invite outsiders to a rehearsal so you can observe their reactions. But then you have to be prepared to interpret their responses—and perhaps turn aside some well-meaning but inappropriate advice. Guests can most often help by showing you which speeches aren't coming across clearly.

Part of the fun of dramatics is that so many people create in concert. During rehearsals you will find your production taking on new dimensions, with the cast contributing invaluably. But if clash arises between an actor's interpretation and yours on a *vital* point, insist—gracefully—on your view.

Always remember that you are the pilot and must exercise leadership. Maybe you have heard the story of the dejected little man who trailed down a Paris street in the wake of a clamorous mob. "Why do you follow that rabble?" a friend called. "I've got to," the little man yelled back. "I'm its leader!" Moral obvious.

To fill in gaps for you, here are some more generalizations about directing:

Main aims are to attract and hold the favorable attention of the audience. You will do both if your actors deliver lines well with adequate and fitting action. This book's plays are realistic rather than poetic or stylized. For them, naturalness is a quality you will be after.

Encourage actors to sound as though they are speaking thoughts rather than patly reciting. Be sure they "punch" those speeches that tell the story. And gear projection to your acoustical needs. Your actors should be heard clearly in the back row of your theater. Try sitting there through a rehearsal. You will find some auditoriums and sets of scenery swallow voices more than others. And some parts of the stage—mostly upstage—require louder speech for voices to carry satisfactorily.

Individual actors tend to concentrate on themselves, their own parts. See that they play *with* one another. Nip exaggerated gestures, wrong facial expressions, ragged timing, mistaken emphases and pronunciations, movements that distract.

"Covering," or one actor's blocking another so the audience cannot see him, is another bogy. Test for it from different sections of the auditorium. You cannot always avoid it, but try to. On rare occasions, covering may be desirable. It can lend conviction, for example, when an actor is faking playing a piano and the music is really coming from off stage.

Keep your play moving at a brisk pace. This means picking up cues quickly, not rushing through speeches! In staging a comedy, you will want your actors to "wait for laughs." This device is treated under Acting.

Fundamentally, action on stage creates a series of pictures. Each important moment should find actors in definite groupings —"good guys" against "bad guys" in a melodrama, for example. Movement consists largely of transition from one pictorial composition to another. Try to make this flow seem so natural the audience never has to think about it.

Now and then you will find your stage picture losing balance because of requirements of the play's story. Sometimes you will want to restore balance by "dressing stage"—that is, by sending an actor over to fill in a too-empty area. His movement should seem motivated, of course.

Check your theater's "sight lines" (audience's range of vision). Frequently portions of the stage are not visible from extreme side seats. As far as you can, make sure that important stage action occurs where it will not be cut off from the view of any of your audience. And remind your business manager to sell the extreme side seats last.

Addenda on rehearsals:

Be considerate of your actors' time. Often the whole cast need not remain through a rehearsal. Stagger arrivals and departures. By the way, remember to arrange matters so that each backstage worker can stay out front and watch a rehearsal from start to finish.

A pantomime rehearsal—actors walking through the motions without speaking—aids in perfecting groupings and movement. If your calendar can encompass it, hold one when the actors know their parts.

It is often worth while to call a light and scenery rehearsal. Here crews iron out details while actors cooperate like movie stand-ins. It is unnecessary to run through the entire play. Concentrate on light changes, scenic aspects.

You might also want to schedule a "costume parade," especially when you are doing a period play.

"Dress rehearsal"—which sometimes is the last of several "dress rehearsals"—is the final one before opening night. Run everything as though this were the real thing. Scenery, lights, costumes, make-up, furnishings, props, sound and special effects —the works. Jot down notes on rough spots. A pox on hectic corrections, though. After the show, mention only details that you think can be adjusted without ruffling anyone's confidence!

By all means rehearse your actors for curtain calls. Usual order (if there is enough clapping!): (a) the whole cast, (b) secondary actors, (c) principals. Sometimes, instead of bows, you will find having all your actors grouped in a pantomime fitting. This book's *Marko Goes a Courtin'* is an instance.

Incidentally, make sure you can employ stage terminology glibly to move your cast about. A new director would do well to brush up on the diagram under *stage positions* in the Glossary. Always use "left" and "right" from an actor's point of view as he faces the audience. "Upstage" and "downstage" mean away from the footlights and toward them, respectively. When an actor crosses a stage "above" someone, he passes upstage of him, "below," downstage. These terms harken back to old-time stage floors that sloped from the rear down to the front.

When directing the plays in this collection, refer to the Notes on Staging for specific help with each.

All right, then. You know you have to apply yourself to direct. Luckily, it is pretty hard to fail. Directing relies so heavily on intuition and intangibles that few can challenge your production. Indeed, presentation of the same play by different people—even experts—will more than likely differ radically.

With each directing experience come added know-how and assurance. Actually, the best way to learn is to do. Your errors as well as your home runs will make you more able. But many hits and no turkeys (theatrically speaking) to you!

ACTING

IF only there were a set of rules you could master and zingo! become a superb actor!

Seek no such simple device. Good acting is a mysterious blend of talent, sincerity, ability to take direction, technique got by study and experience, imagination, enjoyment of make-believe, and personal charm.

A hefty list, all right. But no one starts out with all the attributes. They are picked up along the way.

Confidence booster: no telling ahead of time who will make a passable, even a *fine* amateur actor. In any event, you will harvest much from appearing on stage—fun, new friends, a chance to show your mettle before old ones. And not least is a padded poise to carry over into your career and social life.

Another point. Once you have acted you will find yourself observing people more keenly and appreciatively. Sounds trite but you'll see. Forgetting Shakespeare, you will say with the ring of a discoverer, "All the world's a stage!"

And should you aspire to become a professional in the theater, TV, movies, radio—the earlier you start and more you tread the boards the better. Try character parts as well as leads. In fact, grab every part you can land!

Also, work around your little theater in many capacities. Build scenery, make costumes, usher, direct. Notice that you can glean hints on acting from the Directing section of this book.

Here are basic suggestions to help any actor give intelligent performances and feel at ease on stage:

Know the play as a whole and what your character means to it.

Understand why you say and do what you say and do every moment you are before the audience.

Figure out speech, walk, and gestures to suit your role. Through rehearsals strive to develop a convincing portrayal. How? Prescriptions vary. Some savants recommend "losing" yourself in a character, others that part of you "stand aside" in objective control. Whatever your method, what your audience sees should seem the person the playwright conceived.

Realize where your director wants attention focused. By position, gesture, and posture help "point" it. Remember that an actor should be able to stand still, too.

Some important generals and specifics:

For "business," or minor movements, settle on meaningful, true-to-character action—not fidgeting. People talking seldom remain still. Gestures and pantomime add interest, emphasis, humor. You will find essential business written into stage directions. The director will check on anything else you devise, seeing that you fit into the acting ensemble.

It is amazing how crafty but controlled use of commonplace props like a scarf, cigar, or pencil can make a characterization richer. Too, business can reinforce a particular bit of dialogue, another movement, or a situation. It can come before, during, or after a line, depending upon the effect you want.

Ordinarily, speak as you enter; do not wait to walk stage center. Exception: when you are seeking the dramatic value of a pause. A sage trouper's formula advises, "Assume your character two minutes before you enter and ten steps off stage." This means open and close the door in the character of the person you are playing. And act as if you are coming into a familiar dining room, drugstore, or whatever the scene.

How you exit requires care, too. Action on stage has to go on even though you are going off. Often it is good to have crossed to a position near your way out before giving a last line. Then the exit can be quick.

Speak with enough volume and clarity to be understood by the entire audience. This applies even when you are supposed to be whispering or speaking softly. It is usually more difficult to make yourself heard from upstage than downstage—and in some theaters than others. If there are any special acoustical problems, the director will point them out. An elemental principle is to sound at all times as though you have just thought of your lines—not memorized them.

Key plot lines should be neatly stressed. This can be done by a slight pause before them, or special emphasis on enunciation, or a bit of action calling attention to them. Mark the plot lines in your script. And write in any special instructions as well.

While playing any part try for variation in vocal pattern. Do not be monotonous. In some parts you may have to alter your natural manner of speech. Only thumbs down on unasked-for affectation or pseudo-glamour! Characters like the maid in *She Loves Him Yes* would not spring "veddy" or "How have you bean?" By the bye, if your part requires, do not be afraid to look frowzy!

Pick up cues. Acquire a sense of the pace of the play. Do your bit to keep it perking.

Listening is a special art on stage. You break illusion for the audience if you do not pay attention to other actors when it is natural to. Show that you are taking in what you hear. Again, do not overact!

The way you move on stage is important. The body is a vital acting tool. A turn is generally made so the actor faces the audience as he is turning. And when possible, an actor crosses without turning his back to the house. Reason: the face is usually more expressive. When such a turn or cross is plainly awkward or unnatural, forget it.

In sitting or standing, "steal" a bit to keep your face toward the audience. Ordinarily don't cover (block from sight) your fellow actors. Here the director is your guide.

Normally, it is advisable to gesture with the hand away from the audience. Then you do not cover your face. When you talk into a telephone, check that the mouthpiece does not interfere with your projection. Incidentally, in listening to what is supposedly coming over the wire, react but make your pauses somewhat briefer than in real life.

Let no stray movements creep into your acting during a performance. The director has planned where focus should fall and you may detour attention. This applies to necklace twiddling, loosening a collar, mopping a brow, brandishing a hankie, and the like. Such practices are regarded as "scene stealing" and are guaranteed to make you unpopular!

A hint on sitting: do not slouch. Even when relaxed, keep the spine firm so you can turn easily. And so folks in the balcony will be able to see more than the part in your hair!

While on stage, never go out of character to peek at the spectators. *You* are on show.

A knack you ought to acquire when playing comedy is "waiting for laughs." It is a simple matter of timing. As a matter of course, audiences start out wanting to like you. And they grow increasingly cordial when they do not have to stifle guffaws to catch what you are saying. So the trick is to keep them from losing lines or laughs. If they laugh loudly during dialogue, be prepared to stall—or "wait"—a little. After the peak of laughter, but *before* it has died away, pick up again. While waiting, attempt to make the pause look natural. Stay in character and within the framework of the play.

By the way, you can never be sure where audiences will laugh, or how long. One audience finds a gesture convulsing that others have ignored—another sits poker-faced through bits the cast thought sure-fire. In professional theater this unpredictable response helps actors repeat the same role night after night. They relish the creative challenge of "feeling" each house.

Many plays have pre-teen-agers in their casts. If you are chosen to play one, remember an actor can "stretch" to appear younger by (a) the way he walks, stands, gestures, (b) his costume, (c) his make-up. Youngsters are frequently gawky, fidgety, irreverent, somewhat high-voiced, untidy.

Reverse these tokens to seem much older. Take the exuberant bounce out of your walk, mannerisms, and voice. Dress more maturely, use middle-age or old-age make-up. Hop across the years and imagine you *are* older. Nowadays, though, there is rarely reason to act decrepit.

A word about stage fright. Maybe you will feel some. Most professionals do—even famous stars. One topnotcher has confessed his symptoms are "paper bags and butterflies in the stomach, cotton in the mouth, a potato in the larynx, and rubber in the joints." Luckily, you can turn this conglomeration into an asset. Heebie jeebies set your glands to pouring out extra fluids that prime you for a test. The prompter will "throw" you lines if you fluff (do not turn to look at him!). Besides, you yourself can generally ad-lib speeches rather close to the exact ones.

How you can get an A in effort: (a) be on time for rehearsals, (b) learn your part quickly, (c) think in detail about conveying your character, (d) take direction gracefully, (e) do not show yourself in costume and make-up to the assembling audience. If you have an urge to locate private fans, see whether there is a peephole in the curtain. Did you know stock-company players used to reinforce theirs with adhesive to keep it from tearing?

And when the curtain is up, try for a confident, fluent show. After all, it is the actors who get out and carry the ball. Enjoy your job and chances are the audience will have fun, too!

SCENERY AND FURNISHINGS

SO you are the scene designer! If you are new to the job you are probably trying on the title for size. It fits if you go for the exciting, challenging, exhausting (occasionally), rewarding.

Complex theories of scene design flourish, but at the outset you need focus primarily on (a) showing clearly your play's place and time; (b) suiting its mood; (c) evolving a set practical for your group to build and act in.

It follows then that what you put on stage differs from a pure design. Your stage setting helps your actors tell a story to an audience. As ever, in the theater, *the play's the thing!*

Besides working out scenery and furnishings, a scene designer O.K.'s props, costumes, and lights. How much time you put in on these allied matters depends on who is assigned to take charge of each. When a coworker knows more about executing his specialty, he is the expert while you have general responsibility. If you know more, use your knowledge in consultation with him. There is always the director, though, who has final say.

Sometimes you may have to one-man-band it as designer, light man, costumer, etc. That can be done capably, too.

The fact is, scene designers normally find themselves facing far from ideal conditions. Their "theater" may be anything but de luxe—a room, garage, wharf, tent, out of doors, basement, lodge hall, barn. Time, money, and equipment are always more or less limited.

What do you do about shortages? You learn to expect them for one thing. You fall back on ingenuity. You experiment. You compromise with perfection. And outwitting handicaps together has a way of breeding camaraderie in a staff.

Many times your answer will be camouflaging old scenery instead of building new. Sometimes the solution is using minimum scenery or even none at all. A printed sign or an announcer can tell the audience where the play takes place. Maybe your group will want to try theater-in-the-round staging where spectators circle a playing area that holds just props and furnishings.

Happily, the plays in this book lend themselves to simple,

cheap, conventional staging. Your resourcefulness should grow with their doing.

Here is a recommended approach:

1) Read your play and decide on the central idea or theme.

2) Determine what furnishings and props are essential to the action and dialogue. A ground-plan diagram of the set may be provided with your script, just as is done in this book.

3) Take note of the characters' personalities, habits, incomes, background. Also, of the time of day, kind of weather, season of year.

4) Take note of your equipment.

5) And your budget!

6) And the time and number of hands you have for rounding up materials and building.

7) Settle on two or three colors to be dominant. For comedies use warm cheerful hues—red, yellow, orange. Cooler colors— green, blue and purple—fit heavier plays. A neutral gray over a large area can tie a set together. Remember that costumes and lights enter your color scheme.

8) Plan a complete stage set that suits your facilities, including your auditorium's sight lines. Naturally, as you need, modify, simplify, and add to the suggestions in your script. In the main, long, straight lines tend to give dignity, curves lend sprightliness, and sharp angles excitement. A word of caution: minute details on a stage go unappreciated. Theater magic permits you to achieve dramatic values through the power of suggestion. Rely on it!

9) Put down on paper:

    a) What your set will look like. Method may be meager or elaborate. It depends on your artistic flair and inclinations. You can use a diagram like this book's—or a pencil, ink, or color sketch. If you have time and skill, you may even want to make a small model. In any event, it helps greatly to plan your layout to scale.

b) What you can borrow.

c) What you can buy and/or rent.

d) What you have to build.

10) Get the director's approval of your decisions.

11) Confer with the light man and costume head.

12) Give clear assignments to your staff. And look ahead. Avoid the plight of the executive who said he lived his life like a razor—always in hot water or a scrape!

13) If your theater is your workshop, try to smother clatter and chatter during rehearsals. Rule out smoking backstage.

14) Keep up the morale of your staff. They are not going to take curtain calls, but their work is *important!*

What follows will help you in the specific tasks of preparing your set. The Glossary has definitions that supplement the text.

Generally, background or boundary scenery can be divided into two types: (a) drape scenery, made of curtains, sometimes referred to as "hangings," (b) flat scenery, made of flat, cloth-covered wooden frames. Screens fall in the latter category, too.

Which you select is *not* a matter of either-or. Drapes, flats, and screens are often used in combination; you may use any two or all three. Their arrangement can be varied infinitely.

Drapes and flats are not hard to make. Size and shape should depend on stage and sight lines. While they supply locale, they also mask off-stage areas. The theater's own pipes, bare walls, lights, and windows ought to be hidden.

It also pays to keep in mind storage facilities. When you "strike" a set after a play's run, *save* whatever you can. Fresh paint, new arrangement—new set!

Drape Scenery

Drape scenery is the easier type to use. Basic is a set of draperies to surround the playing area. A front curtain comes in mighty handy, too.

Draperies can be made of many materials. Suggested: duvetyn, velour, cotton rep, monk's cloth (best when lined since it drapes well, but stretches), cotton corduroy (more expensive, but it looks like velvet), denim, and unbleached muslin (cheapest) which can be dyed or painted. Rule out very lightweight materials. Hangings need body.

All-purpose drapes are usually gray or neutral in color to set off costumes without competing with them. Then, too, by changing your lighting the color of these drapes can be altered readily. Black drapes are most often preferred in combination with flats, screens, or set pieces (trees, boulders, platforms, flight of steps, etc.). Black will let emphasis fall on whatever is used with it. The front curtain is usually of a striking color—vibrant red, blue, or green. These put the audience in an alert, receptive frame of mind.

To make drapes, sew strips of material together vertically. Count on much extra fullness for graceful effect when hung. Top and bottom hems of about 2 inches are desirable. Place grommets, or metal eyelets, at intervals along your top hem, about 1 inch from the top. The drapes can then be hung by threading a track of wire through the grommets.

Helpful details: weight the bottom of drapes, preferably with a chain, along the entire hem to assure scenery that will stay put. And when joining lengths of material, do not stitch together the first 7 feet from the floor. Instead use snaps to fasten. Then if you want to insert a door frame, fireplace, window, or set piece, you can roll up the surplus section of drapery to accommodate it.

As for your front curtain, it has to be pulled. Some shower hooks through grommets, parallel wires, and a pulley system like that of home drawstring curtains will produce a workable unit.

If for some reason a front curtain is impractical, remember that you can bring up lights to define the beginning of an act, and dim them for the end.

Cyclorama

Here is a good place to ring in the cyclorama. A "cyc" is a curtain, canvas, or wall skirting the playing area. Generally it is semicircular, high enough and broad enough to mask backstage. It is commonly used for the sky of exterior sets, with paint or light lending it a blue cast. When you hang other drapes to define an interior set, it often serves as backing for windows, doors, etc. Some groups with limited funds settle for a cyc as their basic scenery expenditure. Some do without. Another recourse: paint the back wall of your theater so it can assume the duties of a cyc.

Backing

Backing lends perspective to a set. Importantly, too, it limits the view of an audience through openings such as doorways and windows. It may denote sky, tree, darkness, the wall of a hall, another room or house, an orchard, sea, village roof tops, a city skyline, etc. For backing use flats, screens, drapes, or cyc. Backing which rolls or slides up and down is dubbed a "backdrop" or "drop."

Building Flats

Flats consist of light frames of lumber with canvas or muslin tacked on one side. The canvas gets painted, the flats lashed or hinged together and propped from behind so they will stand in place. Presto! You have the confines of a room, camp bunk, or what need you.

Here is a blow-by-blow description of how to build flats:

Realize, first of all, that a certain degree of exactitude has to be respected. Try to measure carefully. Square corners. Finished pieces should fit together without gaps.

A standard flat is 12 feet high by 5 feet 9 inches wide. If these dimensions do not suit your needs, alter them! But notice that 12 feet. While a shorter height saves time and money, scenery should do more than brush the crowns of actors' heads.

Best to use is 1- by 3-inch white pine. Sugar pine, spruce, and fir are next-bests.

Cut your top and bottom pieces exactly 5 feet 9 inches long. These are called "rails." The upright pieces running vertically between the rails are "stiles." Cut them so that when joined to rails the over-all height is 12 feet. Secure the joints by hammering a few corrugated fasteners (standard hardware stock) across the seams.

Fit a 1- by 3-inch piece across the center. It is termed a "toggle bar." Add two diagonal corner braces—often made of 1- by 2-inch lumber—from a stile to the top rail, and from the same stile to the bottom rail. Reinforce the joints with sturdy three-ply veneer board. The three-ply veneer is usually cut into triangles, called "corner blocks," for the four corners. It is cut into keystones for the toggle bar and into half-keystones for the diagonal braces.

Some carpentry basics: use clout nails or screws to fasten the corner blocks and keystones. Screws are more easily removed if the flat ever has to be altered for future use. With clout nails the tips should be clinched, or turned back into the frame, for nails

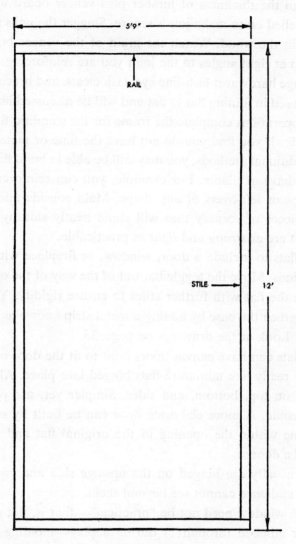

5'9"

RAIL

STILE

12'

FRAME FOR STANDARD FLAT

longer than the thickness of lumber plus veneer board are customarily relied on to make joints secure. Stagger the nails so they do not split the wood. Watch the grain of the veneer board. It should run at right angles to the joint you are reinforcing.

Add stage hardware: lash-line eye, lash cleats, and brace cleats. They are used in joining flat to flat and will be discussed later.

These operations complete the frame for the standard flat.

An aside: if you find you do not have the time or materials to follow traditional methods, you may still be able to build flats with what you have available. For example, you can reinforce joints with scraps or left-overs of any shape. Main consideration is to achieve pieces of scenery that will stand neatly side by side— pieces that are as *strong* and *light* as practicable.

Make flats to include a door, window, or fireplace with some modifications. Move the toggle bar out of the way of the opening. Reinforce the flat with further stiles to ensure rigidity. You can also strengthen the base by adding a metal strip known as a "saddle iron." Look at the drawings on page 33.

Door flats can have canvas doors built to fit the door opening. These are really like miniature flats hinged into place. Allow for clearance on top, bottom, and sides. Simpler yet, use portieres where feasible. A more elaborate door can be built by setting a door frame within the opening of the original flat and using a replica of a door.

Doors usually are hinged on the upstage side and swing off. Then the audience cannot see beyond them.

When a window need not be "practical"—that is, not opened, closed, or climbed through(!) during a play—molding around the aperture in your flat will create an adequate illusion, especially with some curtains—and perhaps a window screen. If you need a practical unit, insert a sturdy frame in the flat opening.

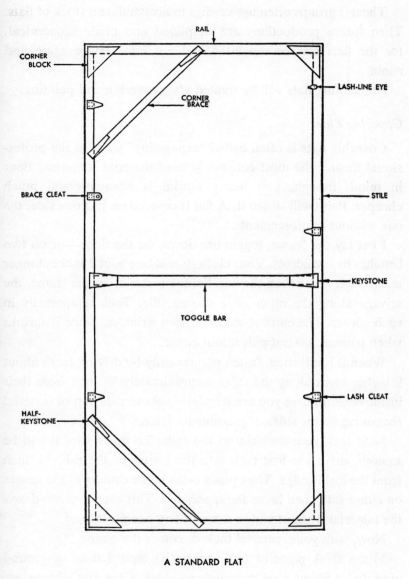

A STANDARD FLAT

Labels on figure:
- RAIL
- CORNER BLOCK
- CORNER BRACE
- LASH-LINE EYE
- BRACE CLEAT
- STILE
- KEYSTONE
- TOGGLE BAR
- LASH CLEAT
- HALF-KEYSTONE

Theater groups often use savings to accumulate a stock of flats. Then future productions are simplified and made economical, for the flats can be repainted and put into service again and again.

Assembling flats will be treated after covering and painting.

Covering Flats

Covering flats is often called "canvassing" since in the professional theater the most commonly used material is canvas. Bear in mind, though, that heavy muslin is adequate and much cheaper. Paint will stiffen it. A flat is covered on just one side, the one without reinforcements.

First lay the frame, toggle bar down, on the floor—or on two benches or sawhorses. Your cloth should be about 3 inches longer and 1 inch wider than the flat. Set the material on the frame, the selvage along the outer edge of one stile. Tack temporarily in each corner. The cloth should not have wrinkles. Since it shrinks when painted, do not pull it taut either.

When it is adjusted, fasten permanently by driving tacks about 9 inches apart along the stiles, approximately ½ inch from their inside edge. In case you are wondering about that flap of material remaining on the stiles, it gets glued—later.

Next tack your material to the rails. To make sure it will be smooth, drive the first tack into the center of the rail, ¼ inch from the inside edge. Then place tacks in the centers of the spaces on either side, then halve the spaces left. This even division draws the material without undue stress in any one place.

Now, with your material tacked, comes the gluing.

Mix a thick paste of (a) water, (b) melted flake or ground glue, (c) whiting, a white powdered chalk. Glue and whiting are found in paint and hardware stores. The flake form of glue is

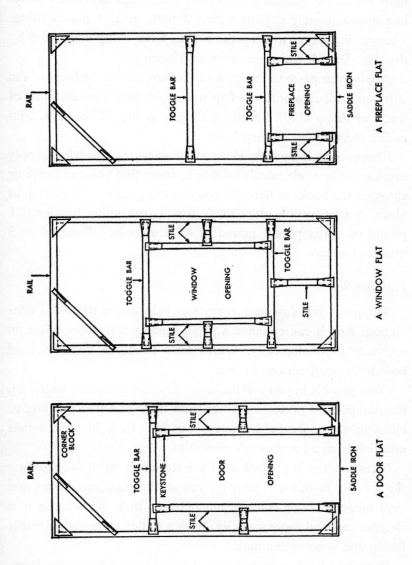

A FIREPLACE FLAT

RAIL

STILE

TOGGLE BAR

TOGGLE BAR

FIREPLACE OPENING

STILE

SADDLE IRON

A WINDOW FLAT

RAIL

TOGGLE BAR

STILE

WINDOW OPENING

STILE

TOGGLE BAR

STILE

A DOOR FLAT

RAIL

CORNER BLOCK

STILE

TOGGLE BAR

KEYSTONE

DOOR OPENING

STILE

SADDLE IRON

more expensive than the ground, but has greater adhesive quality. Use approximately 6 parts water, 2 parts glue, 1 part whiting. The whiting serves to keep the canvas from being discolored by the glue. Danish whiting is most satisfactory.

Apply your paste to the back of the flap and to the faces of the stiles and rails. Smooth the flap into place with a small block of wood or damp cloth. Set the flat aside to dry. When it is, trim excess canvas with a sharp knife.

Fireproofing is a worth-while safety measure. Theatrical supply firms sell special chemicals soluble in water that you can brush or spray on the backs of flats. Or you can use a saturated solution of alum. A preparation often made for flameproofing lumber is 1 pound of borax plus 1 pound of sal ammoniac, dissolved in 3 quarts of water.

Painting Scenery

The paint you dab on scenery can help create theatrical conviction. And it can enhance a play's mood since colors affect an audience psychologically. Warm hues reinforce comedy, cold ones underscore serious drama.

Once you dig in you will find even a novice can paint a set well, for standards of perfection differ from those in house painting or close-up work. Be bold. Sweep—suggest. Etch in only details effective from an audience's viewpoint.

Most scenery is painted with a water-color paint prepared on the job. By blending it yourself you attain more exact hues and save money. Water color is much better than oil because it is cheaper, applied more speedily, gives a duller (in a good sense!) finish, and is not inflammable.

In making your scene paint combine (a) paint in powder form, (b) water, (c) size water, usually known as "size." Size is a mixture of thin flake or ground glue and water. It acts as a binder and prevents paint from scraping off. More details shortly.

The pigment you will use most often is whiting, the same white powdered chalk enlisted previously in gluing the flap of a flat. Other popular dry paint hues are yellow ochre—a dull yellow, venetian red—a brownish red, burnt umber—a dark brown, chrome green—a rather bright green, ultramarine—a blue, and drop black—a standard label on a paint-store shelf.

You will rarely achieve the exact shade you want without blending two or more pigments. Mix them together dry. It is trial and error. Keep track of proportions so you will come very close to repeating yourself—precise matching is well-nigh impossible, as every painter knows—if you run short. But try not to. A big way out: mix too much paint rather than too little. One gallon of paint should cover at least one and one-quarter average flats.

Two-thirds of a bucket of dry color gives a full bucket of scene paint, for you add water. Stir well to dissolve the powder thoroughly.

To make size, the recipe's third ingredient, buy flake (preferably) or ground glue in a paint or hardware store. You have to bring the glue to liquid consistency to blend it into the paint. Maybe you are wondering why everyday glue is not used. Mostly, it is too expensive. Also, it tends to change the color of the paint.

Let two-thirds of a pail of glue stand a few hours—overnight, if you can—with some water covering it. Then set the pail of glue in another larger pail containing a few inches of water. Place this double-boiler combination on a stove. A small, portable electric stove is mighty handy for the purpose. By the way, do not let the water boil out of the bottom pail. This may seem obvious—but!

In about twenty minutes the glue will resemble molasses in consistency. That means it is size and ready to use. Since size hardens when cold, use it warm. One pound of glue yields about four gallons of size.

Now you add size to your mixture of dry paint and water. Quantity: about one-half cupful of size to one gallon of paint. Stir well. The end product should have the thickness of hot fudge sauce. Apply it warm.

Test your scene paint by dabbing some on a swatch of canvas. Let it dry. If the color rubs off, you need more size. If the canvas puckers and cracks, you have used too much. Trial and error again, but it is easier to correct too little size than an overdose. Incidentally, scene paint has a way of drying lighter in color than it looks at first.

A good brush to use is a house painter's wall brush with 4-inch bristles, the solid-bristle type.

Spread your flats out on the floor. Or hang them if you have the equipment. Begin by applying a first or "prime" coat of paint. This readies the surface for other coats. Put it on fairly evenly. Whiting—which is the cheapest pigment—makes a good base. Let it dry. Your next coat should hide it.

Here is an odd fact about brushing on that next coat. You will get better results by making strokes in all directions rather than keeping them parallel.

Once the color background is on, spattering paint of yet another color on top creates a more interesting illusion theater-wise. Flatly painted canvas looks like just that to an audience. But when the texture is varied somewhat, your effect becomes less monotonous and—much more convincing.

To spatter (in your old clothes, of course!), dip your brush in paint. Wipe it off on the side of your bucket. Stand about a yard from the flat, your left side toward it. Strike the handle of the brush against the palm of your left hand. A shower of paint snapped by your right wrist will land on the flat in small spots. Freckle the entire surface in this manner. Be generous, but do not make blobs.

Choose the color you spatter in relation to the effect you want. The more allied the background and spatter coats, the smoother the texture of the surface will appear. Sometimes several colors can be spattered, and stage lights can single out the one you want dominant for any given scene.

Paint may be treated imaginatively to suggest brick, wood, rock, tumbling plaster, adobe, etc. Work in cahoots with the light man, for lighting helps greatly in achieving your illusions.

Bear in mind that flats can be repainted, used again. When applying another coat of paint, do it quickly with a minimum of brushing. Then water in the new coat will not dissolve size in the old and make the two coats mix. Some splotchiness may ensue anyway, but usually not enough to matter on stage.

Keep your courage about you in all this activity. Dare to experiment. What looks crude close up will take on an entirely different aspect at a distance, under stage lights. If painting fascinates you, take note of cause and effect. Every painter for the theater accumulates his private file of trade secrets!

Assembling Flats

Until needed, flats are stored as individual pieces. To create a set, they are hinged or lashed together with rope and propped up from behind with braces. Hinges give more rigidity than rope, but demand finicky alignment.

Simple stage hardware helps the assembly. It is usually put on when a flat frame is built. You can buy this hardware from a theatrical supply company, where it is inexpensive standard stock. Or work with substitutes.

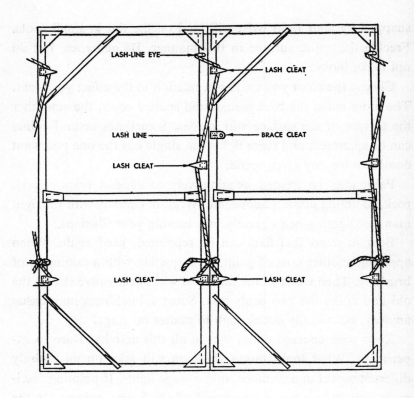

LASH-LINE EYE

LASH CLEAT

LASH LINE

BRACE CLEAT

LASH CLEAT

LASH CLEAT

LASH CLEAT

A WAY TO LASH FLATS

A lash-line eye is used for fastening the top of a lash line. The rope is then slung around lash cleats to bind two flats (6-penny nails are possible fill-ins). A brace cleat has a hole to accommodate a stage brace. It, too, can be used as a lash cleat. Recommended for secure lashing: No. 8 sash cord.

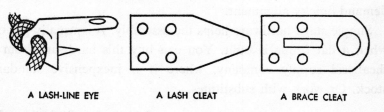

A LASH-LINE EYE   A LASH CLEAT   A BRACE CLEAT

Use a stage brace to support a flat in the middle of a long wall, or at the edge of a set, or at vulnerable points like doors and windows. The brace can be placed at any desired angle. It is made of two pieces of wood that slide so you can adjust the length. One end of the brace has a hook that loops through the hole in the brace cleat. The other end has an iron that gets screwed to the floor with a stage screw or "peg."

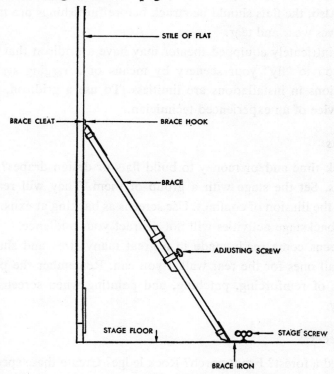

In a pinch, a sturdy length of lumber can be used in place of a stage brace. It can be nailed to the stile and to the stage floor.

When your flats are set up, check your sight lines, particularly from the more extreme side seats. An audience is not supposed to see downstage edges of flats or overhead lights. Where possible mask sides and tops of flats by hanging drapes or, if your theater has them, by using "teaser" and "tormentors."

Mark proper positions of flats and furnishings on the stage floor if you need to strike a set before a show or shift scenery during one. Number your flats on the back to speed their assembly, and keep them in order.

As a rule, furnishings and props should be set on stage before flats. Also, the flats should be struck before furnishings are taken off. Saves wear and tear.

An intricately equipped theater may have a gridiron that permits you to "fly" your scenery by means of a rigging system. Variations in installations are limitless. To use a gridiron, seek the advice of an experienced technician.

Screens

Lack time and/or money to build flats or design drapes? Try screens. Set the stage with a group of them. They will readily create the illusion of confines. Use screens as backing at exits, too. Then backstage activities will not distract your audience.

Screens come ready-made in a great many sizes and shapes. Pick tall ones for the rear wall if you can. Remember the possibilities of reinforcing, patching, and painting when screens are rickety.

Set Pieces

Need a forest? Front porch? Rock ledge? Create these speedily with set pieces—detached units of scenery. Stand a tree (made in your workshop from chicken wire and painted canvas) before a drape, and you have a forest. For stage purposes, note, one or two trees *can* make a forest! A platform can denote a front porch, throne dais, rampart and so on.

Lumber, scrap and good, crates, branches, chicken and other wire, profile (three-ply veneer) board, muslin and canvas, papier-mâché, plastics, paint, miscellaneous hardware, all—attacked with ingenuity—will yield fine set pieces. No rules here. If it satisfies you on stage, it is right.

Furnishings

Furnishing an amateur show is mostly a matter of borrowing and improvising. That is because suitable pieces are usually around to be mustered and worked with. You can rent, you can buy, but it takes m-o-n-e-y.

Keep your eyes open in trotting about town for likely sources: stores, second-hand furniture dealers, salvage societies, specialty shops, other theater groups. Cull from the homes of crew, cast, and friends. Be trustworthy about returning. A reputation for reliability pays off concretely. So, sometimes, does a policy of issuing courtesy passes to merchants who prove obliging.

Improvisation is part of the bewitchery of doing plays. You will have fun amassing "grouplore" like how you made a luxurious divan out of crates and aged shower curtains, the prow of a canoe from a wheelbarrow.

Inspect all furnishings with safety in mind. If a piece is shaky, reinforce it to avoid accidents.

Since borrowing will probably glean unrelated pieces, count on spending time making them conform to stage plan and color scheme. Remember that tones clashing in real life often are harmonious on stage. And that cheap material or remnants can make passable slip covers—passable from an audience's viewpoint. Also, that battered furniture can look natty enough after polishing, and with the addition of tablecloths, scarves, and antimacassars. Your job is to integrate the miscellaneous.

Do not waste time and energy on custom details and subtleties that make rooms in homes seem nicely decorated. Audiences respond to broader units and effects. Examine a set from mid-theater. You will quickly spot inadequate areas. Remedies will suggest themselves.

The plays in this book make few demands of you. After each there is a list of basic furnishings. By all means supplement with anything your stage—or the director—needs.

For period plays and foreign locales do some research. A simple way to treat their furnishings is to rely on a few key pieces to carry the scene.

Wrap Up

With a little practice scenery and furnishings can be prepared and handled with surprising ease. For special problems seek advice from experienced persons. If no one is available, turn to the library. Many times a relevant book—there are manuals on every phase of stagecraft—will help you find your course.

Always on your side is the spell cast over spectators when house lights are down and the curtain is up. Audiences are ready to go along with your illusions, however stylized or skimpy your make-do's. As in all phases of stagecraft, be inventive. With but one watchword: *help the play!*

PROPERTIES

SO you have been chosen prop man!

You will find there is no fixed boundary between properties and furnishings. Usually props are items actors handle during a play (luggage, dishes, food, money) or that adorn the scenery or furnishings (a portrait, flowerpot, telephone, tablecloth).

Give lots of thought to your props. They can do ever so much to lend authenticity and help set the time and place of a play.

Start out by reading the script. Once you are familiar with the play, go through it listing every prop. Then discuss your list with the director. He may have some specific requirements, or hints—or may simply tell you that you are on your own.

Frequently the actors will agree to round up the personal properties they handle during the play. But you have to check up on them, and also collect all the rest.

Borrow, buy, rent, make. When your play calls for an esoteric prop that might take real ferreting, try planting an appeal in the newspaper and on bulletin boards. Example: "There's a dire need for an old-fashioned crystal radio set with earphones at the Hillview Theater." Often an approximation of the prop, or a substitute, will do admirably. Be resourceful.

All props should be assembled by an appointed rehearsal, and the earlier the better for the cast's sake. Sometimes it is tricky for an actor to learn to synchronize a prop with his speech and gestures. And on opening night you don't want one flubbing like James Thurber's witch who "was riding a whirlwind and got caught in the tree and lost my broom and woe was me."

Get the scene designer and director to approve your props. Also, if they add any during rehearsals, you must supply them.

Before the curtain goes up and during the course of the play, proceed with a sense of unflurried order. Props have to be *where* you want 'em, *when* you want 'em, *how* you want 'em. Actors have a way of being completely absorbed with their looks and their lines. They are depending on you to supervise the properties.

Establish a routine for placing the required props on stage before each performance. Show your actors exactly where they will find the ones they are supposed to bring on with them during the play.

Then, between rehearsals and throughout the run of your show, safeguard all properties. Some theater groups keep a cabinet with a trusty lock backstage for this purpose.

Once the show is over, you return all borrowed and rented props, and store away the ones the group owns.

To speed your work with this book's plays, each has a property list and specific hints in the Notes on Staging.

COSTUMES

DO you dress the figures you doodle? Are you nimble with a needle—or at least with pins? Then you should enjoy being a costume head.

The plays in this book are in modern dress. They are easy to clothe. But costuming any show profits from creative thought. "Right" costumes make major contributions. Not least is the visual enjoyment they bring.

Costuming asks an eye for fabrics, color, design. There is little one-two-three about it. Begin by reading your play, penetrating each character, and savoring costume possibilities. When you dovetail with other production departments your plans may change. But first, let your mind roam. Conceive sweeping stage pictures with your actors in appropriate dress.

"Costume," of course, is an inclusive term. Besides garments, it covers shoes, stockings, gloves, hats, jewelry, other accessories. Each ensemble should be all of a piece.

For many plays actors can assemble their own outfits. Family closets and storerooms are lush hunting grounds. Whatever they round up, naturally, has to pass your approval. You may have to supply finishing touches or do some revamping.

Other times costumes are made, improvised, borrowed, bought, rented—by you, under restrictions of treasury, time, and number of assistants. Occasionally you will feel like a wizard, converting the what-you-have into the what-you-need. Remember that your ally is the will-to-believe an audience brings to the theater.

After you have read your play and considered the general style of production, you may want to sketch costume ideas. What matter, of course, are your concepts of line and color, not your art work. Note that long, straight lines tend to suggest dignity, severity. Curves convey a sprightly spirit, and sharp angles are jolting, exciting. Colors count dramatically too.

Some guide posts:

Plan all your costumes thoughtfully to harmonize in color and spirit with the scenery, for they are a part of stage design. Get your ideas O.K.'d by the director and scene designer. Definitely confer with the light man, too. He can wash out your colors and fabric-effects. If you are not sure what lights will do to materials, test samples.

As a rule, light of a hue similar to a costume's (like a blue light on blue) picks it up, heightens brilliance. And light of a complementary hue (like amber on blue) flattens, dulls.

Use colors strategically to point up emotional values. In general, dress sympathetic characters in warm hues—red, orange, yellow. That way your audience is led subtly to favor them. If you go further and make the tones of their costumes harmonious, they will be associated instinctively, and the play will be strengthened.

Reverse twist: clothe unsympathetic characters in cool colors —blue, green, purple—again, to a degree. Here you are motivating spectators to root against them and, because of related hues, to link them with one another.

Antagonists can wear colors that clash. This underlines conflict.

As you proceed, you will find colors need not be mingled as discreetly as in real life. A vivid, dramatic note can often be struck by flamboyant combinations in a costume that would shock your friends on a date. Caution: actors should not wear colors too discordant with chairs they sit in or the scenic background.

If you cannot find the shades you want in ready-made fabrics, draft dyestuffs. They are cheap and practical working tools. Follow directions on the dye package. Try a sample first if you have doubts.

Keep in mind that you can fake on materials. Use inexpensive substitutes that drape and fold as they should and look a proper weight and texture. The professional theater rarely sacrifices the effect of actual velvets, silks, brocades, voluminous folds, and the like. Willy-nilly, you may have to—and with little loss. Try cotton flannel for velvet, plastic for satin. Rummage through yardage departments. Feel materials. Ask questions. Experiment.

Maybe you have not thought of this just because it is so obvious, but it is *important*. Costumes help an audience keep players straight. Do not make them monotonous!

Costumes help actors establish quickly certain recognizable characters—flirts, fops, fuddy-duds, for example. And they are great assets in every kind of characterization. Have them fit the personality type as well as the body, dominating neither unless a script calls for it.

Costumes have to allow essential freedom of action. While remaining true to style, they ought to leave actors as unfettered as possible.

Let your costumes clarify much for an audience. They can serve to convey historic period, geographic locale, time of day, kind of weather, season of year. They can help tell characters' ages, occupations, incomes, habits, social positions. And they can be factors in expressing the type of play (comedy, tragedy, farce, etc.), the style (realistic, romantic, symbolic, etc.), the mood (majestic, satiric, drab, etc.).

Apply the same principles you do to everyday clothing to make costumes accentuate—or tune down—height, girth, dignity, and beauty. They can even reduce an actor's self-consciousness! By throwing attention on his stage personality, they may induce him to intensify his actions and speech, get "into" a part, and feel confidence.

Note on shoes: you may remember Walt Disney's "Dopey" who prompted the plaint:

> Somebody's shoes are squeaking again;
> Pick him up and carry him, men!

Squeaky footwear is an abomination on stage!

To arrive at authentic foreign and period clothes, do research. Consult books, magazines, paintings, photographs. Observe drape and length of skirt, cut of sleeve, waistline, type of fabric, ornaments. Do not go overboard on details, because you may swamp your play or actors. Just convey the dominant features of style. By the bye, it is surprising how much incidental information costume heads pick up. Ever hear of a liripipe, for instance, or a dhoti?

Remember that many cities have reliable costume-renting firms. They can save long hours of sewing.

A good preliminary in making a costume is cutting a pattern. Frequently a standard pattern can be modified to suit your needs.

Incidentally, you may find it helpful to thumb through pattern catalogues for useful style details.

In general, use lots of machine sewing rather than intricate hand stitching. Arrange for fittings. Above all, make fastenings and seams secure. No actor can give his best when worrying about shedding!

If you have time, schedule a "costume parade." Let your actors appear in costume, and both you and the director examine them critically. The actors will appreciate the chance to get the "feel" of their garments.

Whenever cumbersome garb or trappings are planned—like a bustle, hip boots, or clanking armor—urge players to practice with approximations. Introduce the real items at rehearsals early as possible.

By dress rehearsal everything should be ready. Director, stage crew, light and make-up men—all will be checking results at the same time. But if you spot need for costume alterations, pitch in soon as you can lay hands on garments.

At times actors can be made responsible for safekeeping their own costumes. Otherwise, work out a system for storing them between rehearsals and between performances.

See that costumes look fresh for each show. Ironing board and iron can be lifesavers backstage. Double-check snaps and buttons. Parenthetically, it is good policy to clean borrowed apparel before returning.

Save any costumes you make. They may come in handy for later plays. And tuck away in your mind perceptions you arrive at. They often can be put to use in your daily living, and at earning one, too.

MAKE-UP

MAKING up for a part? In charge of make-up for a production? You realize there is more to it than stage-happily masking with goo.

Theatrical make-up has three good reasons for being used: (a) to make actors look their parts, (b) to counteract the power of stage lights to wash out complexions, (c) to make features clear to the back rows of the audience.

If feasible, all make-up should be tested before dress rehearsal. This way, tendencies to overdo and underdo can be caught and amended. Opening night will benefit, for everyone will be used to his make-up and to seeing the whole cast camouflaged.

After a make-up meets approval, jot down what has been applied where. Then repeating comes easy. And you know how much time to allow.

For this book's plays, with most roles straight young adult, make-up needs are simple. Main aim is to enhance the actors' features. Matter of fact, grease paint is never an absolute must. You can work with large doses of ordinary cosmetics—or go without.

And yet—stage make-up is not very costly. Its effect is splendid, even psychologically. And it lasts a long time. If you can afford it, be sure to buy some at a well-stocked drugstore or theatrical supply house.

Acquire cold cream, face powder, grease paint (a few shades), lining pencils or "liners" made of small sticks of grease paint (a few shades), rouge, lipstick, crepe hair, spirit gum (an adhesive mixture of gum arabic and ether), cornstarch. You will also need cleansing tissue, powder puffs, a soft brush or rabbit's foot, mirrors. By the way, supply firms sell special kits fitted out for beginners.

Always remember that every face deserves individual consideration. Each has unique bone structure, wrinkles, hollows, and padding. Adapt generalizations to the face you are making up.

Here is how to put on a straight young adult or "juvenile" make-up.

Begin with a clean skin. And for men, a freshly shaven one. Rub a light film of cold cream over forehead, eyelids, cheeks, nose, and chin, and all around the neck. Wipe off the cream thoroughly with tissue, leaving surfaces barely moist. With palms or finger tips smooth on a grease-paint base. Stroke upward and outward. Choose a color designated for juveniles.

Grease paint, note, comes in skin tones ranging from clown white to Indian red. Shades can be combined. On men the foundation should verge more toward sunburn than pink.

Blend grease paint over the skin evenly. Incidentally, it will hide mild skin eruptions. Thin off as you approach clothes to escape soiling. Better yet, if practicable, put on make-up before costumes.

Dab wet rouge on the cheeks. Exact position depends on the contour of the face. It looks wider with bright spots farther apart. Girls' rouge should start rather high on the cheekbone and fade out by mid-cheek, achieving something of a triangle with base on top. Men's rouge should begin at a lower point and blend out at the jawbone. It should give them a healthy rather than a feminine look.

Avoid islands of red. It helps to touch earlobes and rims with a bit of color.

Now to the eyes. They are acting aids and you will want to accentuate them. Treat both alike or you may wind up with a "cock-eyed" effect!

To darken eyebrows, use liner itself or dip a thin stick (toothpick, orange stick, matchstick, etc.) into it. Apply sparingly—a light shade of brown for fair people, deeper for others.

On the eyelids, rub eyeshadow or blue or gray liner. Make it darkest in the center—with gradual shading. Next draw lines with liner close to the eyelashes on the upper and lower lids. These fringing lines should slant together about one-quarter inch beyond the outer corner of each eye.

Girls' eyelashes can be painted with mascara or liner. Add a tiny dot of rouge to the inner corner of each eye. This is often omitted, though it tends to brighten the eyes.

Lips should be shaped clearly with lipstick, red liner, or wet rouge. You can magnify or minimize. Be sure there is a grease-paint base on any lip surface left unrouged. A man's lipstick should be put on discreetly—in a muted shade.

At this point examine the make-up. Check from ear to ear, hairline to costume line. Has anything been overlooked?

Lastly, set the make-up with powder. This increases naturalness, absorbing the grease and preventing shine. Liberally, with puff or cotton, press in—don't rub—a shade matching the base. Whisk off surplus with a soft brush or rabbit's foot. If powder has dulled colors too much, add dry rouge and touch up the eyes.

Best test of a make-up is how it looks on stage under lights. Close up it may seem grotesque, but only if it still looks that way past the first few rows of the theater does it need toning down. Try this trick: sit back from the mirror and narrow your eyes. You will get a passable impression of how the make-up will look from a distance.

Here is a procedure for making a young person appear middle-aged.

Since age sits lightly on many folks, generally go easy. Begin with a clean face. Use cold cream, then a ground tone labeled "middle age." It is paler than juvenile grease paint. Apply rouge and lipstick, normally less vividly than for juveniles, using a deeper shade. Accent eyes—with restraint.

Wrinkle your forehead before a mirror. Smile. Those are your natural lines, the ones the years will etch. Basic in any face are creases on the forehead, at the corners of and between eyes, under cheek muscles, and around the mouth.

To depict middle age (also worry, ill-humor, sickness, villainy, vice, etc.), line *some* of these wrinkles.

First trace brown or gray liner lighthandedly in the grooves you have chosen to stress. Some like a thin brush for this purpose or a stump of pointed rolled paper. Parallel each line with an adjoining one of white or light yellow liner. These "highlights," as the light lines are called, emphasize the furrows and help create the illusion of prominences and hollows. For crow's-feet, trace a network of gray liner around the eyes. Caution: wrinkles look ludicrous if they are overdone. When in doubt, soft-pedal.

Now dust on, and brush off, a powder related in shade to the make-up base.

A sprinkle of cornstarch or aluminum powder is fine for turning hair gray. Often applications at the temples only will do.

Many plays have elderly roles, though there are none in this collection. For old age—as always—begin with a clean face and cold cream. Make the grease-paint base sallow unless robustness is specifically asked for. Rouge cheeks and lips very lightly. Line and highlight more wrinkles than for middle age, placing some on the neck, lips, and hands, too. Shadowing cheeks delicately in gray will suggest hollows. Whiten hair with cornstarch. Leave eyeshadow off lids or use light purple.

Character parts are individual problems—in make-up and in actor psychology, too. Do not be afraid to blanket native charms. Observe people in real life resembling a character and reproduce significant details.

Resort to grease paint, putty, false hair if you wish to transform nose, chin, and eyebrows. You can also simulate scars, block out teeth, style hair. But discretion is the password. Remember to avoid caricature except where desired. Note that a facial area toned a little darker than a foundation will seem depressed, one painted slightly lighter will stand out more.

Artificial crepe hair helps out in many a part. This is a braided, woollike rope sold by the yard in all hair shades. When ordering it, remember that facial shrubbery tends to grow a bit lighter than the crop on the head.

For mustaches and beards: complete all make-up except the false hair. Leave areas where it is to be mounted free of grease paint. Otherwise, spirit gum—your adhesive—will not stick. It helps to outline the exact space hair is to occupy before beginning the make-up process. One way is to hold hanks you are going to use to the face and to trace around them.

Make the mustache or beard by cutting the desired length from the rope. A little goes a long way. Unbraid it, comb it free of kinks. You will have to dampen it and stretch if you are after really straight hair. Shape approximately the way you want, thinning and trimming with scissors.

A mustache should go on in halves, with a slight free space in the declivity under the nose. This is so it will not hamper speech or bob around. Put spirit gum on the upper lip. Also put a speck on the crepe hair if it is new. Let the gum grow tacky. When it is almost dry, press the hair in place. Moisten your finger tips so they will not stick, and use a damp cloth in applying pressure. When the hair is set, comb, twist, and trim precisely. You can wax to make it retain shape. Do not yank at stray hairs or you may undo the works!

Beards should go on in several pieces, following the natural path of hair growth. (Reminder: hair does *not* sprout all the way to the ears!) Spread on spirit gum. Attach two side pieces along the cheeks, then one under the chin, then one on the front. Let these sections overlap. Fill in. Mold as you desire, and trim.

Great diversity in beards is possible. For a period play investigate the customs of the time. You will lend authenticity to the entire production.

Ready-made mustaches and beards can be bought—at a price. For quick changes you may find them preferable.

Tufts of crepe hair make eyebrows shaggy and sideburns long. They will do well for Eliot's goatee in *She Loves Him Yes.*

For an unshaven effect rely on grease-paint liner. Dark-haired men should spread gray or blue lightly along shaving areas, others brown.

Try styling hair to suit roles before resorting to wigs. And work with switches. Besides cornstarch and aluminum powder, copper dust, various powders, mascaras (including white, gold, and silver), and rinses answer for coloring.

Order wigs, if they cannot be sidestepped, from theatrical supply firms. Watch especially how you join them to foreheads. For naturalness, allow no break in tone between skin and wigband.

Men ought to get necessary haircuts at least three days before performance date. A new-mown look is undesirable. Girls should discuss hairdos with the director.

Placement and color of stage lighting strongly affect make-up. Check results under it. For the same type of role in another play you may have to alter make-up if the lighting is different.

Keep costumes clean. Shield shoulders with towel or cape while cosmetics are going on. Bind hair back, too.

Remove make-up right after a show. You will conserve skin health. First off should be false hair. Alcohol will dissolve the spirit gum. Then spread cold cream on generously. Wipe away layers of paint and powder with tissue. Follow up with soap and warm water.

Make-up, mind you, is an expansive subject. Imagination and practice will channel scores of effective routes for you. Never be becalmed by theory. Sail in!

LIGHTING

DO you say, "Make mine lighting"?

Even with limited time and equipment a light man should find his role fascinating. Lighting is one of the least dogmatic elements of stagecraft. Yet it fuses (no pun!) them all.

Caution: see that an electrician checks the lighting system if it is improvised. Avoid fire hazards and obey fire laws! Be firm about having only the light crew handle apparatus.

Let us dive into the functions of lighting. Basically, your lights make the acting and setting *visible* to an audience. Lighting can also impart a degree of naturalness to your scene, especially if it seems to be coming from logical sources. What *are* logical sources? For an outdoor set, the sun, moon, street lights, light shining inside a house, and so on. For interiors, light can seem to originate from lamps, fixtures, or from the outdoors, filtering in through windows, doorways, etc.

But of course true naturalness is *not*—repeat, *not*—a goal. More desirable is the aura of Theater with a capital T that stage lights bring forth. They boost the power of the acting. They give dramatic punch to your scenery, costumes, and make-ups. And then they can direct attention, help change scene, show passage of time, establish mood, sharpen meaning. Subtly, in a measure, they control the show.

A crowning paradox: unless lights are too glaring, or irritatingly dim (or cues are muffed!), an audience will not think about them particularly!

How do you go about lighting a play?

First, read your script. Stay alert to what lights on the whole can do for the setting, actors, mood, and meaning. And look for specific clues that motivate lighting. Meanwhile, keep in mind your facilities, budget, and store of electrical know-how.

Specific clues cover references in dialogue and stage directions to (a) hour of day, season, weather, shadow; (b) how sunlight and moonlight enter a scene through windows, doorways, foliage etc.; (c) artificial sources of light like lamps, gas jets; (d) changes in lighting.

Confer with the director and scene designer. Both may have definite plans and needs. Costume and make-up chiefs may like a powwow, too.

On to execution. Your job is to arrive at which lights to use— where to place them—what colors to assign them—when and how to change them. Combinations of amount, distribution color, and control can vary greatly for the same play—and still be tiptop. Recommended guide: trial and error!

For most plays try for a balance of illumination on set and

actors. Shadows should be faint, and actors' faces, particularly, free of unwanted ones.

Get balance by testing. Turn lights on and off, increase and decrease wattage, try different colors, interchange units, move them nearer and farther from your stage. But balance is not a synonym for dull uniformity. And there are times when strong shadows can create vivid dramatic effects. Here is trial and error again, this time used to achieve unbalance.

Think your experiments have settled your lighting? Hold up! Try it on the actual set and people. Put actors or stand-ins on stage. Now check—and adjust. The director and maybe the scene designer will want to work with you at this point. As you run the gamut of your equipment, they pass judgment.

What if—as sometimes happens, worse luck—it is the eleventh hour and set and costumes *still* are not ready? Undauntedly, wangle samples of their colors and set your lights with them.

Once everything is agreed upon, make a "light plot." Memory is not reliable enough. Put down on paper the position of your lights, their wattages, colors, and cues for changing them. Lists do fine as long as they account for each unit. Old-hand technicians like to draw diagrams of the stage for placement of lights and paths of beams. They also graph dimmer readings.

Practice with your helpers for smoothness in picking up light cues. Poor timing breaks the mood of a show. Ever watch an actor flip a switch, walk away, and umpty-umpth seconds later light flood the stage? That is not for you!

If there is time, the director will probably schedule a light rehearsal. Here the cast walks through its action and emphasis falls on lights, on their effect and efficiency. In any event, dress rehearsal should find your crew fully prepared.

(Incidentally, this book's plays offer few lighting problems.

They are set indoors and do not have elaborate demands. But some do ask illumination of separate areas. In *She Loves Him Yes* and *A Party Is Born* note how lights help change the scene.)

About your equipment: stage lights are usually stationed so they are not seen by an audience. Four types are used most. Poke around a theater to get to know them. They are:

1) "Foots" or footlights. Foots are commonly a strip of household-sized bulbs inside reflectors. They run along the front of the stage floor, casting light up and back over the stage in general. They tend to blend and balance other illumination and to reduce shadows. They are frequently wired in more than one circuit to permit variation in number and color.

2) "Borders" or borderlights. Borders are striplights rigged overhead in rows that parallel the foots. Their light comes down over the general acting area. Depending on depth, a stage normally has from two to five rows of them. Borders, too, are often wired in several circuits so intensity and color can be changed readily.

3) "Floods" or floodlights. Floods are essentially high-watt lamps, from 500 to 2,000 watts, inside reflectors. They are usually mounted on portable stands with adjustable height and angle of focus. Floods can spread illumination over one large area of a stage. They are often used to throw light onto a set through a doorway, window, etc.

4) "Spots" or spotlights. A spot's beam passes through a lens at the opening of its reflector or holder. Thus, its light is concentrated on a specific area where it singles out a person or object. Spots, like floods, are usually flexible in height and angle of focus and are often located off stage on portable stands. Sometimes they are found attached to the proscenium and/or balcony. Convert a flood into a spot by inserting a lens, and vice versa.

"Baby spots" are junior versions of spots. They are good where you need intensity under 500 watts, or where larger instruments cannot be mounted or concealed. A baby spot is frequently the originator of a stream of sunlight through a window. Sometimes one is hidden in a footlight trough.

Some of the above equipment is probably available to you, perhaps all. Maybe your budget or ingenuity will allow you to supplement. Lighting firms *rent* units. You will find their addresses in classified telephone books and theater-magazine ads.

Hints for extemporizing:

An auto headlight or searchlight can be enlisted as a spot.

Many types of cheap, metal reflectors are adaptable for stage use with ordinary high-watt bulbs. If your treasury asks coddling, make them of bread pans, funnels, or wooden troughs lined with tin.

You can buy floodlight bulbs with a silver reflecting surface sealed inside. These dismiss need for other metal backing.

Leaf through mail-order and lighting-firm catalogues. They will suggest ideas. A camera shop is often a source of practical apparatus.

Consider using incidental lights on stage as part of a set. They offer excuse for variety in levels of illumination. Lamps, fireplaces, and other apparent light motivators should hold low-watt bulbs shielded so they do not glare at your audience's eyes. Meanwhile, primary light, of course, comes from foots, borders, etc.

As for control of light, devices can vary from pulling a plug from an outlet to barely perceptible dimming on a de luxe switchboard.

If you are lucky and have a central control board, grow familiar with its knobs and nuances. If you are without one, wire your lights in circuits one person can handle from a station surveying the stage. Or else post assistants at switches and outlets to answer cues or prearranged signals.

Seeking a way to change level of illumination gradually? Turn small bulbs on or off one by one. Your results can be A-one. By the way, dimmer or dimmerette units for regulating brightness are sold by stage lighting companies. For most small stages, a round plate noninterlocking resistance-type machine of 1,000-watt size does amply.

Do not overcomplicate your scheme for governing lights during a show. The trimmer your system, the less chance of slip-up.

Color, along with amount and distribution, is a controllable of stage lighting. Tints change a set amazingly. Watch how they bestow atmosphere, variety, believability, beauty. Plain white light is rarely used, for it tends to destroy theatrical quality and to flatten tones. But one white spot on a performer can lend extra emphasis when all your other lights are colored.

Introduce color by fastening tinted sheets of gelatin or cellophane before white lights. Gelatin is cheaper and comes in a much wider range of colors. Buy it from a lighting firm. Cellophane is stronger, longer lasting, and obtainable in the five-and-dime. But it is inflammable. See that it never comes in direct contact with a bulb. A space of at least two inches is advisable.

Hold gelatin or cellophane sheets in place with frames. These often come ready-made with stage lights, sliding into prepared grooves. You can improvise frames easily with cardboard and paper clips. Colored bulbs are possibilities. But they are much less flexible, more expensive.

Be versatile with color sheets. Call on two or more thicknesses of the same shade if one allows passage of too much light. Combine colors for just-right hues.

Most commonly used colors are ambers, yellows, pinks, reds,

blues, violets. White frosted gelatin is handy for reducing the brightness of a light.

Rely mostly on warm colors (red, yellow, orange) to light a comedy. They help produce a cheerful feeling. Choose cool tones (blue, green, purple) to establish somber moods for heavier plays.

The colors assigned to lights depend largely on the scenery and costumes. Color appears brightest under lighting of a similar shade. Throw green on a green dress and it will seem startlingly green. Light of a complementary color (blue on orange, for example) dulls intensity. Your lights, then, decide which colors are picked up, especially on backdrops that have been spatter-painted with several.

Remember that colors need not be static. Alter by turning lights on or off. You can also slide superimposed color sheets in or out. Sunrises and sunsets are often made to progress in this manner.

Some particulars: light colors (lemon, straw, steel blue, etc.) make for least change in natural hues. Pink light flatters the complexion. Pale blue does well for sky, daylight blue or blue-green for moonlight. Amber creates sunlight. Green trained on a face is eerie, grotesque. Vivid red can be unearthly, garish.

This discussion has simplified. Color is a convoluted—and exciting—subject of many dimensions. Advice to a novice: investigate, experiment, ree-lax!

The light crew usually mans the house lights—or those for the auditorium proper. Know your curtain cues, correct switches, length of intermissions.

One way to keep *your* face from being red: before each performance make sure your equipment is in working order!

Parting word: let your voice be heard when your group has

banked a profit on a show. Suggest buying lighting equipment. Aside from making life easier for you, it is a fine group invest, ment!

SPECIAL EFFECTS

WIND, rain, sound and fury: Special-effects Man, you create them!

Some plays need you, many do not. Usually the stage manager or prop man fills in on simple assignments.

Requirements of shows, of course, differ endlessly. Your job is to be ingenious—to contrive sounds and effects that work in *your* theater.

Some ways and means:

Phonograph records are basic reliables. One of your group members may own a disk adaptable to your show. You may be able to make a record of sound effects you want. And there are firms (locate them through telephone books and theater-magazine ads) with record libraries catalogued for stage needs. One company advertises it can supply anything "From a Cat's Meow to a Lion's Roar . . . a Pistol Shot to a World War." A particular strain of music, crowd noises, birdcalls, nature in any of its moods—all may be projected via the backstage record player.

Mark your platter at the exact spot you want. Use chalk, white ink, or tape. Then practice so you can cue in with finesse. Make sure your volume is sufficient for your theater. Play into a microphone if you fear the sound will be lost.

Does a bell ring in your play? A record will serve here, too— other expedients as well. An actual bell, for instance! A hardware salesman or an electrician can show you how to wire batteries and a bell or buzzer if you are unfamiliar with such contraptions. Or you can use an alarm clock or bicycle bell with suitable timbre. And you can always tap a knife against a glass for a musical bong. If your script needs several janglers (like a front and back door-bell and telephone), keep rings different. If your theater has a real telephone backstage, consider asking the operator to ring it on a cue from you.

A chime is a good bet for a front door. Merchants will often loan a display model. Then, too, a xylophone can imitate one.

Loud crashes can be managed with a "crash bag"—a canvas or muslin sack holding fragments of glass, tin, rocks, etc. A sealed bag is preferable to a box because the contents will not scatter.

Rain sounds can be concocted by shaking dried peas or beads in a box, or by dropping them on a drum. Set your box on a rocker if downfall is to continue for some time.

The noises of wind are often created by a "wind machine," usually a gadget that rotates a cylinder with wooden slats against a taut cloth. Your theater may have one. Substitutes: running a vacuum cleaner, or posting crewmen off stage to whoosh and whistle.

Another use for a vacuum: to simulate the sound of a motored vehicle.

A "thunder sheet" may come in handy. It is a metal sheet hung backstage where it can be shaken or struck to give off rumbles or loud noise.

Incidentally, the sound man at a radio station may be willing to contribute pointers, lend equipment.

Visual effects—aside from those achieved by lighting—are your domain too. For falling snow, showering white confetti is standard procedure. Drifts may be blown past a window or across the stage by an electric fan. If an actor must stamp on stage covered with snow, use damp salt which can be brushed off realistically. Cotton batting gives the illusion of snow on the ground. Though the ads do not tell you, cornflakes and other dry cereals are good for reproducing the crunch of snow underfoot!

Visible rainfall is tricky. This is because control is mighty important. Try spray from a nozzled hose or a perforated pipe suspended overhead. Arrange to carry away the water, probably by means of a floor trough, and see that your lighting apparatus does not get wet!

Simulate the dance and "play" of fire by hiding a fan under kindling. Then tie bits of gauzy, flame-colored material to catch your breeze.

Occasionally a prop must seem to appear, vanish, or move under its own power. Some scripts contain special instructions for you. Otherwise experiment with string or wire manipulated from off stage, a trap door, a false-topped table, or any convincing optical illusion.

Check that your devices are working before each performance, and strut your brain progeny at *exactly* the right moment. Yours is a department that builds legends. Make them success stories!

PUBLICITY

If you're giving a show
Let people know!

IT is fundamental. Plays are meant to have audiences. That is how a publicity man fits into the picture. Your well-aimed publicity speeds the word.

Also—let's be crass—audiences bring money into the till. You want to meet expenses, maybe show a profit. Naturally, to the cast and crew, your play may seem irresistible. But you know realistically that other entertainment, things-to-do, and lethargy are rather keen competitors.

Plans not yet jelled? Swing your group to performance dates that do not conflict with other crowd-luring events.

Now to mapping out a publicity campaign. Exploit imagination, psychology, and thoroughness. They are your stock in trade.

Seek outlets reaching a tidy share of your potential public. Remember that you do not want all the world; you will compromise—you just want to sell out! Puff your product, making it sound attractive and a good buy. Stimulate curiosity with piquant copy and photos. Shout about it if profits are to go to a worthy cause, if refreshments or dancing will accompany your show. Time news releases to sustain interest, to build to a climax on opening night. Even follow up productions with a story about how good business was.

Be resourceful. Good taste, yes—modesty, no. Adopt tried ballyhoo stunts that still spurt life. Invent others. Your play text may suggest new wrinkles. Example: a great hullabaloo might be made about Marko (really a frog) of *Marko Goes a Courtin'* in this book. "Who's MARKO?" "Have *you* seen MARKO?" "Anyone know where MARKO is?" Take it from there.

Many media reach out to the public. Be discriminating in deciding which are feasible for *your group*.

Newspapers are particularly influential. Editors generally cooperate when releases are written so that they have news value. Should any not see print, do not shy away from submitting more. Space is short some issues, not others.

Build releases around your choice of play, tryout schedule, results of casting, chatter on the author and actors. When human interest details crop up, treat them engagingly and send them along. Ingenuity can embroider stories, but out-and-out hokum is not likely to rate space.

Never assume readers absorbed earlier stories. Every release— *all* publicity, as far as practical—should contain clearly your "who, what, when, and where." This last covers both theater location and places tickets are sold. Ring in "why" if doing a benefit. To survive cutting, the five "w's" should make the first paragraph. Take pains to spell names (*drawing cards!*) correctly. And include information about the price of tickets.

Pictures are eye-arresters. Send photos (glossy prints) to the press—portraits of actors, in or out of costume, scenes from the show. Insert the "w's" in captions.

Advertising in newspapers is nearly always effective. But ads cost. Can your budget take it?

Handbills, stickers, and banners offer chances for real originality. Handmake them if job printing is too expensive. Use comedy, intrigue, color, common sense. Plaster telephone poles, bus stops, and locker rooms if local rules do not forbid these tactics.

Exhibit posters—in store windows, schools, libraries, churches, community centers, and clubhouses. Displays of pictures, cartoons, costumes, stage models, books often prove ticket-sellers.

Floats, parades, sandwich men in costume, vehicles with signs, and perhaps sound equipment, are some outdoor "adverteasers." Airplane skywriting is impractical—on windy days!

Make announcements at assemblies and meetings. Ask time to act out brief previews à la movie coming attractions.

Postcards may bring results, particularly if your public is scattered. Such direct mail flatters—but its cost must be weighed against the restricted number reached. Sometimes phone calls work.

Television and radio can serve you, too. Give details to local commentators for free plugs. You may even snag a bid to do a bit from your play! Try spot announcements—if you can afford them.

Along with publicity staff drumbeating, rely heavily on cast and crew. Remind them that "vervy reports and elations bring in friends and relations." In the theater word-of-mouth advertising is extremely—but *extremely*—potent. They should talk-it-up!

It is often sensible publicity-wise to distribute passes. To reviewers, civic officials, recreation and theater leaders, editors who have obliged. But that "comp" list mustn't grow 'n' grow.

The publicity man is often called upon to edit programs. You will find them treated under Business Affairs.

A tangent: toot your group horn discreetly in theater lobby displays. Mount pictures of present and past productions, reviews, clippings. Future shows scheduled? Start the ball a-rollin' again by posting blurbs and dates!

BUSINESS AFFAIRS

BUSINESS manager? Your files reflect the entire history of your show. And "There's no business like show business"!

Of course your functions depend on a project's scope. Usually you monitor the funds, agilely balancing the budget. You keep track of financial arrangements and pay bills. You bank the income from ticket sales, program advertising, donations, and whatever.

You are not only super-responsible, you are hard-boiled—about extra expenditures. If a technician unleashes a brilliant idea that will incidentally overspend his allowance, try to lead him tactfully to a substitute. You love art, but you are black-ink minded.

About tickets: know your theater's layout and capacity. Scale admissions to cover expenses but draw customers. Print date, curtain time, cost, and name of auditorium on your tickets. If seats are to be reserved, include row and number too.

It is often strategic to sell tickets at several places. A centrally located store may allow you part-time facilities, perhaps even vend for you. Booths in school corridors, pitches at club meetings, door-to-door canvassing are bring-'em-ins. A trusty device: make each group member responsible for selling a quota of tickets.

Keep tab on how tickets move. You want to avoid that last-minute wail, "But I thought they'd been sold!" A group should fix rules on passes, issuing them possibly to V.I.P.'s and outsiders aiding production and publicity.

Box-office personnel needs briefing on public relations. Good humor, patience, helpfulness win friends.

Footnote: hoard the experience you gain doling out dollars and dealing with people. It will serve you well when you are economizing for a business or a family!

Programs

Programs dignify a show, lending a degree of permanence to your efforts. Many a playgoer saves his a lifetime!

Program editor's check list: playbills should give title, playwright, director, cast (usually in order of appearance), time and place of scenes, length of intermissions. And, do not forget to credit crew heads and members. The playbill should acknowledge donations and loans of goods and services, too.

Have you "patrons"—people who have come forward with

funds, service, advice or vital moral support? Consider listing them—with permission.

There is great leeway on program format. Print, mimeograph, type, handwrite, what you will. Advertising space is often saleable. The revenue can prove immensely helpful!

Round off the program with notes on the play, actors, group, playwright, coming attractions, names of officers. Mention where your group will serve refreshments after the play if coffee and cider, cookies and doughnuts can conveniently be rustled up. Sometimes you will find inserts like these practical: "Gifts of costumes and stage properties are gratefully received"; "You are invited to come on stage and inspect the set after the play"; "You are urged to add your name to our mailing list for notification of future shows." You might also announce the productions of other groups if they will announce yours in return.

Use taste and strategy in designing your program. Truly, it is a good-will ambassador.

House Management

If you are house manager, you are delegated the host to the theater audience. Not the handshaking kind, but the comfort-conscious variety. The business or publicity man often undertakes the role.

No matter how primitive your arrangements, run the house efficiently. You want a relaxed, secure atmosphere. Ushers should learn your seating plan, carry programs and flashlights, know where rest rooms are, where smoking is permitted. Provide ventilation and heat, if needed. Obey community fire laws.

Anticipate the unscheduled: first aid, lost and found, phone calls, stray children, gate crashers.

Appoint a hostess and committee to superintend refreshments if they are part of your scheme.

Open doors about a half hour earlier than showtime. Be prepared, though, for a rush just before the curtain.

FARE-YE-WELL

WHICH brings us to the point where your audience—even last-minute pour-ins—are seated. This is the moment cast and staff have all been driving for. The house lights dim. The audience is expectant. Curtain's going up! On with the show!

Good luck!

And many happy productions to you!

Belle

A ONE-ACT COMEDY*

BY EDWIN & NATHALIE GROSS

Cast of Characters

BELLE NORRIS	eighteen, attractive, unpolished in manner—not one of the crowd. Fountain clerk in Bowen's Drugstore.
CORA TOMPKINS	the cashier, spinsterish but with a sense of humor.
MR. BOWEN	the druggist, kindly, philosophical, in late middle-age.
YOUNG MAN WITH A VIOLIN CASE	a jaunty type.
NONDESCRIPT MAN	
MRS. HUDSON	tastefully dressed, near forty.
JUDY	about eleven.
NANCY HUDSON	Mrs. Hudson's daughter, a high-school senior.
SUE	Nancy's best friend, a high-school senior.
TED ELLIS	a cut-up, a high-school senior.
JOANIE	cheerleader, a little plump, a high-school senior.

*Adapted from a *Seventeen* magazine story by Genevieve Munson.

GORDON	a bit suave, a high-school senior.
MRS. ELIZABETH DALY	a fussy shopper.
ALAN BIXBY	a college freshman, a snob.
YOUNG MAN WITH	
A CELLO CASE	

PLACE: Bowen's Drugstore in the small town of Fairbanks.

TIME: A Friday afternoon in October.

The scene is Bowen's Drugstore in the small town of Fairbanks. The store is a favorite hangout of the high-school set. Up right center, parallel to the footlights, are a soda fountain and stools. Up left center is a cashier's counter flanked by candy and greeting-card displays. At stage right is a drug counter. Up right is the exit to the pharmacist's section and off-stage telephone. At left are a magazine rack, the store front, and the exit to the street. Two luncheonette tables, with sugar and napkin dispensers, and four chairs around each, are at center. One is somewhat down left, the other more up right.

On the drug counter is a toothbrush display. A sign on the wall at right says "Prescriptions. Licensed Pharmacist." On the cashier's counter are cigar boxes. A telephone book hangs near the street door.

It is a Friday afternoon in October.

As the curtain rises, BELLE NORRIS *is behind the fountain stacking dishes and tidying up. She wears a half-apron over her dress. At the cashier's counter* MISS TOMPKINS *is reading a book. Soon* MR. BOWEN, *the druggist, wearing a white smock, enters up right. He walks quickly to the fountain.*

MR. BOWEN: A cup of coffee, Belle, please.

BELLE: Yes, Mr. Bowen. [*Prepares coffee.*]

MR. BOWEN: You look rather tired.

BELLE: I was up half the night nursing Pop.

MR. BOWEN: Want the rest of the afternoon off?

BELLE: Oh, no, sir. That's all right. Cream and sugar?

MR. BOWEN: Leave it black. [*Shaking head*] Helps an old-timer like me hustle. Sulfa, penicillin, terramycin—seems doctors aren't happy 'less they order them all.

BELLE: [*Smiling*] Here you are, Mr. Bowen.

MR. BOWEN: Thank you, Belle. Now I'll catch up on my prescriptions before some more people get sick. Tell you a secret, Belle. All I ever use myself is aspirin. No wait—bicarbonate too! [*Grins, exits U.R. with cup and saucer.*]

BELLE: Gee, Miss Tompkins, he's a good egg!

MISS TOMPKINS: Best there is in this town—or anywheres. 'Scuse me, I've got to finish this mystery. No sense paying a library fine. Know what? I guessed the murderer before I looked at the last page! [*A* YOUNG MAN WITH A VIOLIN CASE *enters from the street. He looks around the store.*]

Y.M.W.V.C.: Do you have a phone booth, Miss? [BELLE *nods, points off R.*] Thanks. [*Exits, reappears.*] Do you have a phone book?

BELLE: Oh, that's right over there.

Y.M.W.V.C.: [*Quickly consults telephone book and his address book.*] Miss, do you happen to know where Carlyle Carraway lives? I don't see her name listed.

BELLE: No, I don't. Miss Tompkins . . . ever hear of Carlyle Carraway?

MISS TOMPKINS: No, can't say I have. The only Carraways I knew moved fifteen years ago. There was no Carlyle in that crew.

Y.M.W.V.C.: But this girl said she lived here. By golly, this is the town and this is the State! I met her last month when the band was playing Templeton. She said be sure to look her up. Anybody else you could ask? It's—er—kind of important to me.

BELLE: [*Hesitates.*] Well, there's the owner. [*Calls.*] Mr. Bowen! [MR. BOWEN *enters.*]

Y.M.W.V.C.: Sorry to bother you, sir. Just blew into town with the band. Elks dance tonight, you know. I'm looking for Carlyle Carraway. Do you know her?

MR. BOWEN: Young man, I fill prescriptions for everybody in this town—but I've never heard of her.

Y.M.W.V.C.: [*Flippantly*] Maybe she doesn't get sick. Look. Do you know a blonde about five feet one . . . and—[*Wolf whistles.*]

MR. BOWEN: [*Abruptly*] I am here for *scientific* consultation, only. Good day. [*Exits U.R.*]

Y.M.W.V.C.: Brrr! [*Shrugs shoulders, exits L. A* NONDESCRIPT MAN *enters from street and crosses to cashier's booth.*]

NONDESCRIPT MAN: Let's have one of those cigars. [*The* NONDESCRIPT MAN *pays* MISS TOMPKINS, *puts unlit cigar in mouth, and saunters to magazine display. Unobtrusively he browses through many periodicals.* MRS. HUDSON *enters from street and crosses toward drug counter.*]

MRS. HUDSON: Hello, Miss Tompkins. [*Frigidly*] Belle, is Mr. Bowen in?

BELLE: Yes, he is. [*Calling*] Mr. Bowen.

MR. BOWEN: [*Reenters. Coming to drug counter*] Good afternoon, Mrs. Hudson. Good to see you. You're looking well. How's Grandma today?

MRS. HUDSON: Hard to say, Mr. Bowen. The doctor thinks we ought to continue the capsules. He'll know in a week whether he has to operate. Did he phone about renewing the——?

MR. BOWEN: Oh, he did. And I've been working on them. It'll be just a few moments before those salts dissolve.

MRS. HUDSON: I think I'll wait, then.

MR. BOWEN: All rightee. [*Calling*] Belle, you'd better take your rest period now. The high-school bunch'll be here soon.

BELLE: Thanks, Mr. Bowen. I have an errand to do for Pop. [*Removes apron, takes purse and jacket from under counter, and exits L.*]

MRS. HUDSON: [*Disapprovingly*] Hm! An errand for her "Pop"! At the Fairbanks liquor store, no doubt. Mr. Bowen, I've been debating whether Nancy should come in here when that girl's working for you. I was talking about it with Mrs. Ellis only yesterday.

MR. BOWEN: [*Politely reproving*] Come now, Mrs. Hudson, you're not being very broadminded, are you?

MRS. HUDSON: You know well enough what her father is: a no-good——

MR. BOWEN: [*Sternly*] It's Belle Norris who's working for me, not her father. Mrs. Hudson, we must never forget that each and every individual should be judged on his own merits. Now—have you anything against Belle herself?

MRS. HUDSON: Why, everybody knows she was in that scrape at school last term—with Alan Bixby. That's why *she* dropped out and didn't graduate. No one believed for a moment *Alan* was the instigator——

MR. BOWEN: [*Interrupting forcefully*] Let's be fair. No one ever proved Belle was to blame. Because Alan's father owns half the town, why whitewash——?

MRS. HUDSON: [*Interrupting*] But Mr. Bowen, it's awfully easy to put two and two together. Goodness knows, I'm all for helping the underprivileged—but—well, that girl could be a bad influence! You can't tell me she's the *same* as Alan, or my Nancy, or——

MR. BOWEN: Of course she is, Mrs. Hudson! And it's high time she was treated that way—by all of us!

MRS. HUDSON: [*Slightly affronted*] Really, Mr. Bowen! You sound like my husband on a crusade!

MR. BOWEN: [*Earnestly*] Forgive me if I'm being rude, but I've had a chance to study Belle in the last two months. And she proves to me again prejudice is a hateful, despicable thing. It's ridiculous! Chalking off that girl as bad because her father's a sick loafer. Makes me want to broadcast that when my uncle ran this store he poisoned *twenty-three* customers.

MRS. HUDSON: [*Gasping*] He didn't, did he?

MR. BOWEN: [*Humorously*] At least that many. All lame animals.

MRS. HUDSON: [*Amused she was taken in*] Oh, Mr. Bowen!

MR. BOWEN: [*Earnestly*] Now with Belle. Maybe if the girls at school had been friendlier——

MRS. HUDSON: She never encouraged them.

MR. BOWEN: Well, that chapter is over, anyway. But here I am trying to teach that girl self-confidence—and to stand up for her rights. She's learning fast, I will say that. In fact, I happen to know there's a nice young man. . . .

MRS. HUDSON: [*Snappily*] Humph! No one ever said the girl didn't have sex appeal!

MR. BOWEN: [*Clears throat, changes tack.*] She's a loyal, conscientious worker. Not overenthusiastic, perhaps—but then my ice cream sells itself. [BELLE *reenters store. She goes behind fountain, dons apron and resumes tidying.*] Well, that solution should be about ready. Let me see. [*Exits U.R., returns quickly with two bottles.*] Here we are.

MRS. HUDSON: Don't bother wrapping them. Why, the capsules are a different color!

MR. BOWEN: [*Chuckling*] I thought Grandma'd like a change. They'll match the do-hickey she told me about. That new bed jacket!

MRS. HUDSON: [*Giggles, slipping bottles in purse.*] Oh my goodness! That'll give Grandma a laugh, all right. Well, thanks a lot, Mr. Bowen. Charge it please. And—uh—I don't think you ought to tell anybody else about your uncle and the— [*Whispers*] poison. Some might not understand.

MR. BOWEN: [*Grinning*] Thank you, Mrs. Hudson. Tell Grandma I was asking for her. [*Exits U.R.* MRS. HUDSON *exits L.* JUDY, *an eleven-year-old, enters from street carrying schoolbooks. She bumps into* NONDESCRIPT MAN *at magazine rack.*]

JUDY: Excuse me, mister. [*Studies candy display.*]

MISS TOMPKINS: Can I help you, Judy?

JUDY: I'm looking for the candy in the polka-dot paper. The kind with caramel that lasts so long.

MISS TOMPKINS: I'm all out. You bought the last three the day you went to the movies.

JUDY: Ah, what a shame! Now I have to switch. [*Studies display. Occasionally picks up candy bar, reads wrapper and rejects it.* BELLE *has removed a pin from her dress and is polishing it.*]

MISS TOMPKINS: What's that, Belle? New jewelry?

BELLE: [*Self-consciously*] A—a pin. A fraternity pin.

MISS TOMPKINS: [*Surprised*] Really! From anybody I know?

BELLE: Oh, no.

MISS TOMPKINS: When'd you get it?

BELLE: It came in the mail this morning. [*With pride*] It's a Deke.

MISS TOMPKINS: Well, well! [BELLE *replaces pin on dress.* MISS TOMPKINS *looks impressed and quizzical.*]

BELLE: High-school crowd's late this afternoon.

MISS TOMPKINS: Oh, they'll be here. Practically never miss a day! [*Turning to* NONDESCRIPT MAN] Mister, is there any particular magazine you're looking for?

NONDESCRIPT MAN: [*Politely*] Me? No, ma'am. [NANCY HUDSON *and* SUE *enter from street carrying schoolbooks.*]

SUE: And Nancy, what do you think? Then Mrs. Nichols said this time there'll be *no* make-up exam. Anyone absent must average in a zero.

NANCY: Really?

SUE: And she said, "That includes football players!" Did you ever know a halfback to flunk?

NANCY: Only in the baseball season. [NANCY *and* SUE *stow jackets and books at table U.R.C. and sit at table D.L.C.*] Hi, Miss Tompkins.

MISS TOMPKINS: Hello, Nancy. Your mother was just in.

NANCY: Thanks. I met her down the street.

MISS TOMPKINS: By the way, girls, Mrs. Nichols said the same things in my day. Empty threats! [*Resumes reading.*]

BELLE: [*Brings water to table, wipes table with cloth.*] What'll it be today? Chocolate sundaes?

NANCY: We'll wait for the gang, huh, Sue?

SUE: Let's.

BELLE: Okey-doke. [*Returns to fountain.*]

SUE: [*The following remark, like all others* BELLE *is not supposed to hear, is given in a confidential tone, but not particularly softly since there is a comfortable distance between the table D.L.C. and the fountain. Excitedly*] Hey—did you see the frat pin on Belle?

NANCY: [*Amazed*] No. Honest?

SUE: It looks like a Deke. Guess it isn't, though. See if you can catch it.

NANCY: Wow! If it's a *Deke* there'll be fireworks! [TED ELLIS, *the crowd cut-up, enters from street carrying schoolbooks.*]

TED: Hi, everybody! [*Slaps* NANCY *on back.*] How's my current heart-throb?

NANCY: Ted Ellis, grow up!

TED: [*In mock despair*] Thus endeth a great romance! Bury it and pretend to forget! [*Turns to* SUE. *Brightly*] Sue, old girl, dear old girl, how's my current heart-throb?

SUE: [*Flatly*] I don't know her.

TED: [*Crushed, slumps in chair. Rallying quickly*] Whatdaya-think? I counted 'em—and we've only thirty-one more Fri-days of high school! Let's celebrate. Dutch. [*Slides books under table. Calling*] Belle, make mine a Tin Roof this time.

BELLE: What's a Tin Roof?

TED: You mean to say you don't know? It's the Ellis family spe-cial. All gooey. I'll come over and make it myself. [*Rises.*]

BELLE: [*Doubtfully*] I don't think Mr. Bowen would like that.

TED: Listen, Belle. [*Going behind fountain*] My father did it in his day, my big brother did it—and there's no reason why Mr. Bowen should draw the line at me.

SUE: [*Nudges* NANCY.] Wait till Ted spots the pin. What say we get our sundaes now?

NANCY: Suits me.

SUE: [*Calling*] Belle, would you make our sundaes, please.

BELLE: Okay.

TED: Belle, which is the cherry syrup? And the pineapple? Got to have a dash of pineapple. My old man says this gook never tastes the same without it.

BELLE: Cherry's here—pineapple's down the end. I won't know what to charge you for that one.

TED: In my old man's day it was only twenty cents, but it's un-doubtedly gone up.

JUDY: [*Finally selects candy bar. Glumly*] Here, Miss Tompkins. [*Paying*] I guess I'll have to eat this.

MISS TOMPKINS: I think you'll grow very fond of that kind, Judy. They hardly dissolve at all. [JUDY *exits L. To* NONDESCRIPT

MAN] Mister, are you sure there's no particular one you're looking for?

NONDESCRIPT MAN: [*Innocently*] Oh, no. [MISS TOMPKINS *shakes head and returns to book.* JOANIE *and* GORDON *enter,* GORDON *carrying schoolbooks.* JOANIE *wears a cheerleader's outfit.*]

JOANIE: [*With cheerleader's gestures*] Beat St. Johns . . . CAN DO! Beat St. Johns . . . CAN DO! Who can? Fairbanks can! Can what? CAN DO!!!

GORDON: Greetings, greetings.

SUE: Hi, Gordie.

JOANIE: Hi, kids. That's the new cheer we're springing next week. How you like?

NANCY: Not bad, Joanie.

SUE: It's rather cute. [JOANIE *sits.*]

GORDON: [*Calling*] Make it the usual for Joanie and me, Belle. [*Deposits schoolbooks and* JOANIE'S *jacket on chair at table U.R.C.*] Why, lookit Teddy, ol' boy. You the new hired hand around here?

TED: Nah, Belle's still got her job.

GORDON: [*Moves extra chair to table D.L.C.*] Those botany field trips are killing Bowen's business. Place looks deserted.

JOANIE: [*Dejectedly*] What a life! Do I have troubles!

NANCY: What's the matter, Joanie?

JOANIE: I still say if President Monroe could take a test about the Monroe Doctrine and sign my name to it—Mrs. Nichols would fail him!

SUE: Has she got you down, too?

JOANIE: What a sourball!

NANCY: She's not so bad, once you know her.

JOANIE: You're just a softie. Oh! [*Running to rack*] The new *Movie Horizon's* out!

GORDON: What wasted enthusiasm.

JOANIE: [*Returns with magazine. Rummaging through pages*] I hope they printed my letter to the editor. Ooooh! Here it is! Down here! I'll have to buy a dozen copies!

SUE: Some way to spend your allowance!

JOANIE: Look, members of my public. My name's in print again! [*Passes magazine to* SUE *and* NANCY. *Runs to rack for another.*]

NANCY: It's rather exciting, when you think about it.

GORDON: Don't encourage her. I'll never get her away from her typewriter.

TED: [*Comes to table carrying sundae. Excitedly*] Did you see what I saw? Belle Norris is wearing a Deke pin!

JOANIE: [*Amazed, sitting*] What?

GORDON: No kidding?

SUE: Nancy and I spotted it.

JOANIE: I always thought they were hard to hook!

NANCY: Why, they are! Deke's definitely the best frat at State U.

GORDON: Pretty snooty bunch, too.

JOANIE: She must have found it. No Deke in his right mind would give his pin to Belle. I'll just bet she found it.

GORDON: Yeh, somebody ought to check with the Dekes. If they knew a girl like Belle was flashing their pin——

NANCY: Sh-h! She might hear you!

GORDON: [*Lowering voice*] Well, I think we've stumbled on something. It'll get the town buzzing.

NANCY: Oh, you boys are cattier than women. [BELLE, *carrying tray with sundaes and water, comes to table. Awkward pause*]

TED: [*Pretending discovery*] Say, do my eyes deceive me? What kind of pin you got there, Belle? Frat? Sorority? [*Leans forward.*] It's a Deke! Hey, look, all you no-account lassies, Belle's gone and caught herself a Deke!

JOANIE: Whose pin is it, Belle?

BELLE: Someone's.

TED: Come on, Belle, give. . . . Is it someone we know?

BELLE: [*Laughs. Self-conscious but breezy*] Maybe, and maybe not.

TED: Come on! There are a lot of swell Dekes from this town!

BELLE: [*Noncommittally*] That's true. [*Returns to fountain.*]

GORDON: [*Singsonging*] Belle, Belle, do tell!

TED: [*Also singsonging*] Well, well, c'mon, *tell!* [BELLE *ignores them. The* YOUNG MAN WITH A VIOLIN CASE *enters from street.*]

Y.M.W.V.C.: You people were right. The postmaster didn't know any Carraway girl, either. [*Sits at fountain.*] Maybe that was just her professional name. Make me up a sandwich, will you? Anything'll do. Cup of java, too. [BELLE *begins filling order.*] I eat all the time! You wouldn't think it to look at me. Nerves! Doctor says it's all nerves!

JOANIE: She's an old meanie not to tell us anything.

SUE: Maybe it's Doug Fletcher's pin. I think he took her driving a few times last summer.

TED: You're way off the beam, kid. Doug gave his to a girl in Templeton. I know that for a fact.

GORDON: [*Speculatively*] Well, what other Deke could it be?

NANCY: [*Hesitantly*] Alan . . . Alan Bixby?

GORDON: His father'd break a blood vessel!

JOANIE: [*Hoots.*] Nancy, don't be a goose! Alan ignores Belle since that mess at school.

TED: Anyway, Alan's only a pledge.

JOANIE: I'm going to ask the first Deke I see around this week end.

NANCY: Maybe it's not a Fairbanks man.

TED: Yeah—but the possibilities. . . . Say, there's that new fellow works in the shoe store. He's dated Belle once or twice.

GORDON: I notice who's the authority on dating.

JOANIE: Ted, you're cracked. How could the new fellow be a Deke? I doubt he even finished grade school.

SUE: Well, I think Joanie hit it before. Somebody must have lost his pin and Belle found it.

JOANIE: And she's wearing it to put on airs.

TED: Instead of gossiping, we'd know the truth if we wangled the pin off Belle and looked at the name on the back. A Deke pin's engraved, isn't it?

GORDON: And whom do you nominate to do the wangling, my bright friend?

TED: [*Stumbling*] Well, I mean—gee, one of you girls could get sort of friendly with Belle, and maybe pretty soon she'd take you into her confidence and——

JOANIE: [*Sarcastically*] Wouldn't my mother just love that?

SUE: Mine, too.

TED: Aw, you know what I mean—palsy-walsy talk—girl to girl——

JOANIE: Anyway, who wants to wait that long?

NANCY: We're not being practical.

TED: Okay, okay, leave it to your Uncle Ted. [*Calls.*] Belle. [*Beckons to her.* BELLE *comes to table.* TED *unreels magician's act.*] Ahaa! What ees zis I see before me? My creestal ball! [*Picks up sugar dispenser.*] I look into ze creestal ball. And what do I see in eet? [*Breaking mood*] Dust. [*Blows on dispenser and polishes it with his sleeve. His friends enjoy his play-acting. Resuming role*] Ahaa! Wait! Zere ees a feegure! A girl! Belle Norris! She ees wearing a Deke peen! I look wiz my X-ray eye to ze other side of ze pin. Ahaa! Zere is a name on eet. Leesten, everybody! Ze initials! [*Aside*] Come on, Belle! [*Acting again*] Ze initials! [*Aside, loud whisper*] Hey, Belle, what are they? [MR. BOWEN *enters and goes to counter for wrapping paper. He listens, shakes head resignedly, and exits U.R.*]

BELLE: [*Keeping voice level*] If you want to order anything, Ted, I'll wait for you to make up your mind. Otherwise, I have work to do.

TED: [*Replacing sugar dispenser*] Heck. My crystal ball's all clouded over. Temperamental, just like some people.

JOANIE: You're a card, Teddy Bear. Say—maybe you and I could cook up an act like that for class night?

BELLE: [*Starting toward fountain*] Let me know when you want something.

GORDON: Wait a minute, Belle. [*As she halts*] Gee whiz, be a good sport. You know we're dying to get the dope on the pin.

BELLE: It just so happens I don't enjoy being pumped. And I'm sure my private affairs are nobody else's business.

TED: [*Teasing*] Know what, Belle? I think maybe you don't have a boyfriend in Deke at all.

BELLE: [*A little angry*] Oh, you think I'm wearing this pin to bluff?

JOANIE: Well, have we ever seen him, Belle? What's his name?

BELLE: [*Stiffly*] He's not from this town. And his name wouldn't mean anything to you.

TED: Oh, there'd be no harm telling us his name, would there?

JOANIE: You're wearing his pin so you must want people to know.

BELLE: [*Hesitantly*] Well. . . . [*With dignity*] His name is Williams. Billy Williams.

GORDON: Billy Williams . . . ? Nope. Never heard of him.

TED: William Williams. Sounds like a record stuck in a groove.

BELLE: [*Levelly*] It happens to be Wilson Williams. And I didn't ask for any remarks.

TED: I apologize. [*Brightly*] Anyway, now we can see the engraving on the pin, can't we?

BELLE: [*Coldly*] Isn't my word good enough?

TED: [*A bit abashed*] Oh. Yeah. Sure.

SUE: What's he like, Belle? Will you tell us that?

BELLE: [*Somewhat on defensive*] Well—I don't think I want to. . . .

NANCY: [*Pleasantly*] Please! We'd love to know more about your friend. We're really interested.

BELLE: [*Slowly*] He's thin, dark, medium-sized—and kind of good-looking—at least I think so. Sort of serious. [*At* TED] Not a cut-up.

JOANIE: Does Billy go to State?

BELLE: [*Nervously*] No—he went to school in Arizona. Arizona State or State Teachers—something like that. [GORDON *and* JOANIE *exchange looks.*]

JOANIE: How'd you meet him?

BELLE: He goes to the same doctor my Pop does in Jackson City. I met him there. In the doctor's office.

NANCY: Well, I'll bet he's very nice.

TED: [*Clowning again*] But not nearly as amusing as I am, eh, Belle?

BELLE: [*Lighter mood*] No, thank goodness.

Y.M.W.V.C.: Miss, can I have my check, please?

BELLE: Oh, yes, sir. [*Returns to fountain.*]

JOANIE: [*Lowering voice*] Hey, do you kids believe all that hooey?

GORDON: Not me.

TED: I don't know what to make of it.

NANCY: She might be telling the truth. After all. . . .

GORDON: [*Shaking head*] Only that "Billy Williams." Sounds like the first name that popped into her head.

JOANIE: I read about a mountain in Arizona with that name. Maybe she did, too.

TED: The back of that pin could tell us plenty.

NANCY: I think we ought to pretend we believe her. Why always gang up on her? She's not hurting anybody, and if she wants to feel important for a change—well, I don't blame her.

TED: [Knowingly] The Dekes won't like it!

GORDON: That's putting it mildly. [The five concentrate on eating and looking through JOANIE'S magazines.]

Y.M.W.V.C.: [Accepting check, rising] Thanks. Say, are you busy tonight? [Places tip on counter.]

BELLE: Not interested, thank you.

Y.M.W.V.C.: That Elk dance'll be good. We're playing, remember.

BELLE: Sorry.

Y.M.W.V.C.: [Jauntily] Too bad. Well, there's no harm trying, is there? [Pays MISS TOMPKINS. MRS. DALY enters from street. YOUNG MAN WITH A VIOLIN CASE exits L.]

MRS. DALY: Hello, children.

CHORUS: Hello, Mrs. Daly.

MRS. DALY: Hello, Cora.

MISS TOMPKINS: Hello, Elizabeth. [MRS. DALY crosses to toothbrush display.]

BELLE: [Calling] Mr. Bowen.

MR. BOWEN: [Entering, coming to drug counter] Good afternoon, Mrs. Daly. What can I do for you?

MRS. DALY: Well, Mr. Bowen, it's a toothbrush today. [*Producing brush from purse*] My husband's scrubbed the life out of this one. He says he wants another exactly like it.

MR. BOWEN: Here you are, Mrs. Daly. This is the model.

MRS. DALY: Oh, no, Mr. Bowen. That has a green handle—it won't do. You see, Mr. Bowen, *my* toothbrush is green, and if I bought a green one for Virgil, well. . . .

MR. BOWEN: I understand, Mrs. Daly. [*Rummaging*] Hmm. Most of my stock seems to be green right now. . . . Here. How's this one?

MRS. DALY: [*Looking it over*] No. That has hard bristles. See? "H." This old one says "M." Medium.

MR. BOWEN: Oh, of course, so it does. . . . Well, here we are. This one's a medium.

MRS. DALY: [*Examining it closely*] Umm. [*Frowns.*] Ummmm. It seems to have too much of a curve on top. Right here. Uh! I've torn the cellophane! I'm so sorry! How clumsy of me! [*Places brush on counter.*]

MR. BOWEN: [*Resignedly*] That's all right, Mrs. Daly.

MRS. DALY: I hope I don't seem fussy. I'm not keeping you back, am I? I could look myself.

MR. BOWEN: [*Emphatically*] Oh, no, Mrs. Daly! I'm here to wait on you! That's my job!

MRS. DALY: Maybe you have some under the counter.

MR. BOWEN: Every last toothbrush in the store's right here. I arranged this display at noon, Mrs. Daly.

MRS. DALY: Oh, dear. [*Stands perplexed.* MR. BOWEN *harriedly rummages further.*] Oh, dear.

MR. BOWEN: [*Helpfully*] I'll tell you what, Mrs. Daly. Suppose you take one of these other models home, and if Virgil doesn't like it you can always bring it back. Try to watch the cellophane, though.

MRS. DALY: Why, thank you, Mr. Bowen. [*Suddenly titters.*]

MR. BOWEN: Have I said something funny?

MRS. DALY: Oh, no! I mean—I just thought—I'll leave this old one here with you, and I'll just *bet* Virgil never knows the difference! [*Telephone rings off R.*]

BELLE: I'll take it, Mr. Bowen. [*Exits.* MR. BOWEN *wraps toothbrush, writes sales check.*]

MRS. DALY: Well, thank you *very much,* Mr. Bowen.

MR. BOWEN: You're entirely welcome, Mrs. Daly. Come in again.

MRS. DALY: [*Crosses to cashier's booth.*] I certainly hate to buy a toothbrush for somebody else.

MISS TOMPKINS: It is a responsibility, Elizabeth. [MRS. DALY *pays and exits L.*]

MR. BOWEN: [*Muttering, straightening toothbrush display*] I ought to charge a special fee for advice.

BELLE: [*Reentering*] Nancy, phone call. It's your mother.

NANCY: Thanks. [*Rises and crosses.*] Hello, Mr. Bowen.

MR. BOWEN: Hello, Nancy. [NANCY *exits U.R.* MR. BOWEN *accidentally knocks over toothbrush display. Exasperated, he scoops up brushes. Exiting with display*] I think I'll discontinue toothbrushes! [NONDESCRIPT MAN *saunters out L.*]

SUE: I'm getting just plain sick of chocolate sundaes. How's the Tin Roof, Ted?

TED: Leaky—I mean, super.

JOANIE: I'd order a giant malt, but I have enough trouble zipping this skirt now.

TED: There's the secret of your success, kit. You add weight to our cheers. [*Looking toward street*] Hey, hold everything! There's Al Bixby getting off the bus! Wait a minute, gang! I'll see if I can drag him in here! [*Dashes off L.*]

SUE: Alan must have come for the week end.

GORDON: What kind of football fan is he?

JOANIE: State's playing away from home tomorrow.

GORDON: Look at the frosh hat on the boy! [*Calling out*] H'ya, Big Shot! [TED *and* ALAN BIXBY *enter.* ALAN *swaggers slightly, wears a college freshman hat, and carries a week-end bag.*]

TED: My friends, I give you Alan Bixby, B.M.O.C.—big man on campus himself.

ALAN: Hi, everybody. [*To* TED] Take it easy, sonny. Got a couple of years for that.

JOANIE: Why, Alan, have you turned modest?

ALAN: No-o. But you meet some big men at State U.—especially in Deke.

TED: [*Facetiously*] Part of his initiation, people. The Dekes make pledges go around saying things like that. [*Transfers chair from table U.R.C.*] Come on, feller, sit down. Join us in a sundae, Monday, or what have you.

ALAN: Thanks, Teddy. [*Sits.*] What's new around town, kids?

GORDON: Oh, it's been kind of quiet. Nothing much cooking yet. Guess we miss your gang. [*Lower*] But did you see the hunk of jewelry Belle Norris has on? [*Clicks tongue.*]

ALAN: No.

GORDON: [*Huddling over table*] She's wearing a frat pin. Delta Epsilon Kappa, better known as Deke. She's practically a sister of yours.

ALAN: [*Incredulous*] Are you kidding, Gordon?

SUE: Honest.

TED: You can see for yourself.

ALAN: [*Trying to pass it off*] Well, never know what a brother'll do. Though a pin's supposed to be pretty sacred. [BELLE *starts D.L. with glass of water.*]

GORDON: She gave us a story about some guy she met in Jackson City.

JOANIE: [*Spotting* BELLE *and trying to cover up, loudly*] You know how these things are. . . .

TED: [*Clears throat warningly.*] Hi, Belle. We were just telling Alan about your Deke pin. You and he are practically in the same family.

BELLE: [*Coldly*] Uh-huh. [*Serves water.*] Alan, may I have your order?

ALAN: [*Brusquely*] Skip it. [*Peremptorily*] I want to look at that pin, Belle.

BELLE: [*Startled*] Why, what do you mean?

ALAN: Where'd you get it?

BELLE: A friend gave it to me. Not that it's any of your business. In fact, Alan, it's less yours than anybody else's.

ALAN: Oh, I wouldn't say that. Is this friend anyone I know?

BELLE: I doubt it very much.

ALAN: What's his name?

BELLE: Billy Williams. And don't try to place him. He's from Arizona.

ALAN: Well, that's interesting. I'll look him up in our Deke directory. We have a book with the names of all members, you know. Covers every chapter in the country.

BELLE: [*Tossing her head*] I didn't know. But you look him up, you hear? Wilson Williams. Now do you want to order?

ALAN: No. [BELLE *returns to fountain.*]

GORDON: If it's phony she should've picked a more convincing name. Billy Williams. . . . Bobby Roberts. . . . Eddie Edwards.

TED: [*Needling*] Well, Alan, old chum, I guess Deke's losing its prestige. When I get to State I'll have to pledge Zeta Psi.

GORDON: Yeh, me too. After all, if the Dekes aren't particular about their women. . . .

TED: Yep! Once a frat begins to slip it goes downhill fast. [ALAN *rises abruptly and moves U.R.*]

ALAN: [*Angry*] I'd like to see the back of that pin, Belle. [*Unobtrusively* NANCY *enters U.R. and halts near drug counter.*]

BELLE: Alan, what are you getting at? Look—I've been civil. I've answered your questions. I tell you this was Billy Williams' pin and he gave it to me. Now drop it!

ALAN: Suppose I don't believe you?

BELLE: [*Voice rising angrily*] So what? It's really none of your business. It's none of your business, I tell you! And you'd better leave me alone or . . . I'll call Mr. Bowen!

Belle • 9 3

ALAN: Oh, I don't think you'll call Mr. Bowen. Come on—hand over that pin.

BELLE: [*Distraughtly*] I tell you—this pin—belongs to me! My word should be enough!

ALAN: Okay, maybe I'm wrong. A look at that thing'll settle it once and for all. [MR. BOWEN *appears U.R. He stands behind* NANCY, *listening.*]

BELLE: [*Shrilly*] Listen, Alan, I don't have to toady! I let you wiggle out of a fix once and slip the blame on me! Well, I don't want anything more to do with you or your. . . .

ALAN: [*Venomously*] Give me that pin!

BELLE: I won't!

ALAN: Just as I thought—you're *scared!* Well, I know someone who lost a pin around here. Want me to tell who that pin belongs to? And where you probably *stole* it? [MR. BOWEN *starts forward but checks himself.*]

BELLE: [*Slapping* ALAN's *face*] There! I didn't steal it! Don't you *dare* say I did!

ALAN: [*Standing his ground*] Come on. Hand it over.

BELLE: [*Tightly*] I'd like to—oh, I'd like to . . . ! [*Starts removing pin, trembling with rage.*]

NANCY: [*Springing forward, heatedly*] Don't do it, Belle! Who does he think he is? She didn't steal your darn old Deke pin! And you'd better leave her alone!

ALAN: [*Nastily*] How do you know she didn't steal it?

NANCY: 'Cause—'cause I happen to know the Deke who gave it to her! That's how!

ALAN: [*Sneeringly*] So you know him, huh? How come?

NANCY: Well, I—I know him because he's—er—Belle's—er. . . . [*Swallows.*]

SUE: [*Rising, forcefully*] Sure—sure Nancy knows him! She told me that before!

NANCY: That's right! And if you have any questions, save them for Billy Williams! It was his pin! Now it's Belle's! And that's that!

ALAN: [*Unconvinced but backing down*] Okay. I'll take your word, Nancy. But I'm going to check that Williams guy in the directory. Let it go now, Belle. [*Returns to table. Picking up week-end bag*] Got to scram, kids. I'm not going back till Sunday night. [*Starts L.*] Maybe I'll see you.

TED: So long, Alan.

GORDON: Be good.

MR. BOWEN: [*Sharply*] Alan!

ALAN: [*Turning*] Yes?

MR. BOWEN: [*Scathingly*] You've disgraced yourself! I won't shame you any more in front of your friends! You drop in to see me before you leave town! That's all! [ALAN *exits L.* MR. BOWEN *exits U.R.* NANCY *returns to table.*]

TED: [*Rising. Subdued*] Time we shoved along, eh, kids?

JOANIE: Uh-huh.

GORDON: Definitely.

TED: Belle, can we have our checks, please? [*A feeling of self-consciousness prevails all around.* BELLE *crosses to table, distributes checks, returns to fountain. The five gather belongings.* TED *collects their change.*]

GORDON: I'm paying for Joanie.

JOANIE: [*Jokingly*] Thanks. Are the magazines thrown in?

GORDON: I draw the line!

JOANIE: I'll autograph one for you.

GORDON: Not interested.

JOANIE: [*Blithely*] Okay. [*Adds change.* TED *pays* MISS TOMP-KINS.] Say, want to come to my house for Ping-pong?

SUE: That'd be fun.

GORDON: Good idea. I feel like punishing a ball. [*Strokes with imaginary paddle.*]

NANCY: I have to run an errand for Mom. You kids have a doubles game without me. Sue, be sure you phone me tonight, huh?

SUE: You bet, Nancy.

NANCY: Don't forget.

JOANIE: Okay, gang—let's step on it! So long, Nance.

TED: [*Yelling*] Can do, can do—NO CAN DO! How does it go, Joanie? [TED, GORDON, JOANIE, *and* SUE *exeunt L.* NANCY *finishes collecting belongings.*]

BELLE: Nancy—can I speak to you a minute?

NANCY: Sure.

BELLE: [*Crossing, shyly*] Nancy, I—I want to thank you. It was certainly decent of you to say you knew Billy.

NANCY: Oh, that's all right. You told us about him—so I figured I could say I knew him. Anyway, it was a pleasure to stop Alan.

BELLE: [*Sincerely*] It was still mighty nice of you. Sue too.

NANCY: [*Embarrassed*] Belle, I don't know how to say this, but—uh—wouldn't it make things easier if you didn't wear the pin around here? You know how the kids talk and joke.

BELLE: I know all right.

NANCY: Of course really the pin is your own business—but it's a Deke—and so many families in town feel they own Deke —[*Flounders.*] and—well. . . .

BELLE: [*Understandingly, unclasping pin*] It's all right, Nancy. I'll show you. I hated to give Alan or the others the satisfaction—[*Gives pin to* NANCY.]

NANCY: [*Reading inscription. With relief*] Why, it *does* say Wilson Williams!

BELLE: Sure—and he's my beau, too.

NANCY: [*Glowingly*] I'm so happy for you, Belle. I really am!

BELLE: [*Shyly confiding*] Things have begun to look up for me. Since I've been working here—I feel more as though—I count!

NANCY: I know what you mean. And I wish you lots of luck. [*Returns pin.*] Gee, I've got to run. See you tomorrow.

BELLE: [*Self-consciously*] Do you . . . think you'd like to meet Billy when he comes here?

NANCY: [*Touched and pleased*] Why, I'd love to, Belle!

BELLE: [*Hesitantly*] Nancy, may I bring your grandmother zinnias? My garden has some lovely ones.

NANCY: Of course! Grandma'd love it! Bring them over any time. And thanks.

BELLE: Thank *you!*

NANCY: 'Bye now. 'Bye, Miss Tompkins.

MISS TOMPKINS: 'Bye, Nancy. [NANCY *exits L.* BELLE *clears table.*] Let me tell you, Belle, I kept my peace before, but I was rooting for you.

BELLE: Thanks! [*Returns to fountain. The* NONDESCRIPT MAN *enters from street and goes to magazines.*]

MISS TOMPKINS: [*Sarcastically*] You know, Belle, I think Mr. Bowen should install a turnstile over there. Then that section would show a profit! [*The* NONDESCRIPT MAN *chooses a magazine and reads. A* YOUNG MAN WITH A CELLO CASE *enters from street, address book in hand.*]

Y.M.W.C.C.: Say, Miss, can you tell me where Carlyle Carraway lives?

MISS TOMPKINS: [*Dogmatically*] There's no such person in this town.

Y.M.W.C.C.: [*Incredulous*] Are you positive?

MISS TOMPKINS: I am, young man. No doubt about it.

Y.M.W.C.C.: Gee whiz, that's funny! She told me to be sure to look her up!

The Curtain Falls.

NOTES ON STAGING

BELLE, even though full of fun, has a serious theme. As Mr. Bowen puts it, "We must never forget that each and every individual should be judged on his own merits."

Some of the bang in staging *Belle* comes from showing the

panorama of an American drugstore. There is a flow of people, a sense of broad scene.

Belle's sharp clash of characters leads to tense conflict. Its denouement (theater lingo for outcome) rewards the side of democracy and understanding. The audience goes away satisfied and happy.

By the way, the fraternity mentioned in the play is called "Delta Epsilon Kappa." It is not a real frat, so toes escape crushing.

Acting

To carry *Belle's* climax, the eight players in the scene should rehearse carefully. Ensemble acting takes finesse in timing and attention to movement and grouping. The play's other roles—CORA TOMPKINS, the two young men, JUDY, MRS. HUDSON, MRS. DALY and the NONDESCRIPT MAN—may be classed roughly as "bits" and rehearsed less finically.

In sitting around the table, the high-school crowd should be wary of "covering" (blocking one another from the sight of the audience).

About the characters:

BELLE, the heroine, should seem slightly unpolished—though attractive and sympathetic.

MR. BOWEN is getting along in years. He is respected in town, and his moralizing about democracy carries conviction. Sincerity is important in acting him, and good humor too.

JUDY may be changed to a boy's part if expedient. Or acted by someone older.

Both JUDY and the NONDESCRIPT MAN are on stage for intervals when interest is on others. They should avoid idle fidgeting, since any movement snags attention. It is for the director to indicate when they can draw focus.

The high-school crowd—NANCY, SUE, TED, JOANIE, and GORDON—gossip in undertones about BELLE. But they must project to the entire audience. (Notice BELLE's fountain is up right, a convincing separation from the group's downstage table.) And no speaking with mouths full. There is all the time MRS. DALY is on stage to polish off sundaes.

MRS. DALY is a fussy shopper. Still, she should not be burlesqued. There *are* such people.

ALAN BIXBY is glib, self-confident.

The YOUNG MAN WITH A VIOLIN CASE and YOUNG MAN WITH A CELLO CASE give an idea of the transient trade that wanders through a drugstore. They are obviously alien to town.

Scenery and Furnishings

Belle's set may be involved or not, as you wish. Decide at the outset how much realism you want and can manage. Then inspect your favorite drugstore. Which aspects should be *suggested* on stage, which reproduced literally? Remember that petty details are lost to an audience. If you paint shelves of drugs on your flats, you need not draw trade-marks on bottles. Even your actors will not notice!

For the confines of the store use flats, drapes and/or screens (see Guide).

Borrow trimmings from your druggist. (Take good care of them, naturally.)

Make the soda fountain sturdy. It is sat at, worked behind. Its basis can be a table, a string of cabinets or bookcases, or even a dresser topped by a wide board. The fixture's intricate side (toward the clerk) is never visible, so forget it. The fountain may be rimmed by kitchen or lab stools—and backed by signs advertising current specials.

The cashier and drug counters can also be improvised. As for the magazine display, a bench can be the foundation. The two luncheonette tables should preferably match.

Think about the store front. You can suggest a window by

painting one on a flat (lettering "BOWEN'S PHARMACY" in reverse is a good touch). Or heighten the magazine display, back it with advertising placards, and skip a window. If you are after realism, you can build a broad window with a street scene backing. Might even let the audience see an occasional passer-by through it!

Properties

The toothbrush display should be a movable unit (MR. BOWEN must knock it over). For the sundaes, custard (unfrozen) makes a fine, non-melting ice cream.

Keep props at the fountain simple. The audience cannot see directly behind it, and BELLE and TED work below counter level. But you do need those passed over the counter, plus minimum equipment to keep BELLE busy. For general effect, plant items like a small stove and malted mixer.

Costumes and Make-up

BELLE'S clothes are neat, inexpensive, subdued. Keep her half-apron businesslike.

MISS TOMPKINS looks slightly dowdy but pleasant. Decide for yourself how old you want her, though she should not be ancient. She had a teacher the seniors have now!

MR. BOWEN'S smock can be borrowed from a druggist, doctor, barber. See the Guide for advice on his middle-age make-up.

MRS. HUDSON is tastefully dressed. Make-up should set her near forty.

The high-school seniors wear everyday school clothes. Except JOANIE, who has on a cheerleader's outfit.

MRS. DALY'S get-up can suggest her concentration on trivia. Perhaps her neckline is too severe, or she carries an umbrella, or her purse is oversized, with a formidable array of locks. You can tell at a glance that life is complicated for MRS. DALY.

ALAN BIXBY is smoothly dressed. Only incongruous touch is his freshman cap.

The two musicians should appear flashy.

Special Effects and Lighting

You may want to work in a few off-stage traffic noises—like auto horns, a bus motor starting (a vacuum cleaner will serve).

No specific light changes are asked for in the script.

Suggest the outdoors by lighting the off-stage area beyond the street entrance. If there is a transparent store window, show daylight beyond with a spotlight or flood.

Publicity

Capitalize on *Belle's* locale and diversity of characters for a lively campaign. One group distributed aspirin tablets with *Belle* printed on them. "You won't need one after you've seen *Belle!*" said the drumbeaters.

Belle's theme, too, rates ballyhoo!

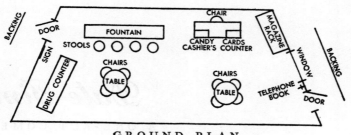

GROUND PLAN

FURNISHINGS	PROPERTIES	
soda fountain	sugar dispensers	two medicine bottles
stools	napkin dispensers	schoolbooks
cashier's counter	toothbrush display	candy bars
cash register	(at least two	fraternity pin
(optional)	brushes in cello-	glasses of water
candy and greeting-	phane)	cloth
card displays	cigar boxes	sundaes
drug counter	telephone book	tray
magazine rack	dishes	wrapping paper (dis-
two luncheonette	library book	penser optional)
tables	two cups and saucers	fountain checks
nine chairs	sandwich	money
sign "PRESCRIPTIONS.	violin case	MRS. DALY's tooth-
LICENSED PHARMA-	address book	brush
CIST."	cigar	sales check
	magazines	week-end bag
	BELLE's purse and	cello case
	jacket	

Date-Time

A ONE-ACT COMEDY
BY EDWIN & NATHALIE GROSS

Cast of Characters

POP MYGATT	explosive but harmless, dogmatic but well-intentioned. In his forties.
MOM MYGATT	his wife, understanding and diplomatic. In her forties.
ALICE MYGATT	their teen-age daughter. Pretty and self-concerned.
BILLY MYGATT	their son. Sociable, pesky, moderately irrepressible. About twelve.
GEORGE HOLLINGSHEAD	Alice's date. Dapper, self-confident, and poised. About twenty.

PLACE: Dining room of the Mygatt family.

TIME: Shortly past seven o'clock on a Saturday evening.

The scene is the comfortable, simply furnished dining room of the Mygatt family. At stage right stand a radio and china closet. At left are a buffet with a baseball guide on it, and further upstage a door leading to the kitchen. Another door, up right center, leads to a hall. Both doors can remain open throughout. Left of the hall

*door are a telephone on a table and a serving table with fruit bowl
and tray. At center is a dining table set with tablecloth, dessert
dishes, cups and a pie.*

As the curtain rises, the MYGATTS *are sitting around the dining
table.* POP MYGATT, *in an armchair up center, is feeling righteous
and picking at his pie absently.* MOM MYGATT *sits opposite him,
wearing an apron over a neat dress.* ALICE, *in an attractive casual
dress, sits at right,* BILLY *at left.*

It is shortly past seven o'clock on a Saturday evening.

MOM *finishes her dessert. She folds her napkin and crosses to
the serving table.*

MOM: How about some fruit, children? [*Returning with bowl*]
Would you like a pear—or an apple, Dad? See, here's a very
nice one.

POP: (*Solemnly*) Nothing else for me, thank you. [*Drums fingers
on table.*]

MOM: Alice? [ALICE *takes pear. Lightly*] How'd your new shoes
feel last night, dear? Were they comfortable for dancing?

ALICE: Oh, yes, Mom. They were fine. Didn't even start to pinch
till we were on the way home.

BILLY: You should have let me break 'em in for you. Why, that
article I read told you 'xactly how to do it. You wouldn't've
known you had shoes on.

ALICE: I wouldn't have had any shoes left!

BILLY: You're a scaredy-cat! [*As* MOM *approaches*] No fruit for
me, Mom. This pie's too good. Make it yourself?

MOM: [*Returning bowl to serving table*] Of course, Billy.

BILLY: If you were thirty years younger I'd marry you tonight—if
I could get Pop's written permission. You need it for every-

thing nowadays. Did you sign that form, Pop? I want to try out for the baseball team.

POP: [*Solemnly*] I did, young man. [*Slaps table emphatically.*]

MOM: [*Solicitously resting hand on* POP'S *shoulder*] Anything troubling you, Dad?

POP: [*Gravely*] There's a matter or two on my mind.

BILLY: [*Blithely*] You can't make pie as good as this, Alice. Did you ever tell George that?

ALICE: Don't be silly. George isn't the least bit interested in my baking!

BILLY: Oh, you're the intellectual type. [MOM *starts to stack dishes. Scraping plate*] Say, can I have another piece, Mom?

MOM: You've had two already. [*Sighs.*] But I suppose so.

ALICE: Now wait a minute, Billy. Didn't you tell me you're in training? If you eat so much pie you won't even make the second-string.

BILLY: You've got a point there, Alice. Think I'll pass it up, Mom. [*Rising*] I'll eat it for breakfast. [*Exits U.R.C. Sticks head back in, remembering manners.*] Excuse me. [*Disappears R.*]

MOM: Thank goodness the first one was a girl. [*Begins clearing table, using serving table tray.*] We can still make the early show, Dad.

POP: Not interested, Amy. I've some other plans! [*Nods in* ALICE'S *direction, fiddles with cigar.*]

BILLY: [*Returning U.R.C. with newspaper*] Alice, see this ad for the Hotel Pickwick? The floor show sure sounds swell. [*Sits.*]

Oughta get George to take you there some night. You could make it after a movie, or something.

POP: It seems to me that George—uh—what's-his-name has enough ideas without you butting in, young man. What *is* his last name, Alice?

ALICE: Hollingshead, Dad.

POP: Hmmm. [*Flicks studiously at crumbs of pie on tablecloth.*]

BILLY: [*Turns page.*] Pop, you saw Babe Ruth play, didn't you?

POP: [*Grunting*] Uh-huh.

BILLY: Show me how he used to get up at bat, Pop. Show me how he used to address the ball.

MOM: [*Lightly*] *I'll* show you, Billy. Your father isn't in the mood. But you'll have to give me time to practice with a broomstick.

BILLY: Gee, Mom, you're cute. Isn't she cute, Alice? What do you say, Pop?

POP: Haven't you homework to do, young man?

BILLY: Aw, Pop, it's Saturday night. If you did homework Saturday nights, I bet Mom never would've married you.

POP: Why your great interest in matrimony this evening? Don't tell me you're going steady with anyone . . . the way some other people seem to be?

BILLY: Oh no, Pop—my allowance is hardly enough for one.

POP: Good. I hope you're learning to hold on to your money, Billy. [*Pointedly*] Certain young men who come to this house seem much too free with theirs.

MOM: Dishes don't get done just looking at them! [*Exits L. with tray.*]

ALICE: [*Hurrying with pear*] I'll be right with you, Mom. [POP *flicks crumbs off his vest. Rising*] Excuse me.

POP: [*Gravely*] Please stay here, Alice. There's a little matter I'd like to discuss with you.

ALICE: [*Sitting*] But Mom's expecting me to help with——

POP: Never mind. The dishes can wait. [*Short pause. With innuendo*] I heard you come in with George last night. [BILLY *pretends to be buried in newspaper.*]

ALICE: [*Embarrassed, weakly*] Oh, you did, Pop?

POP: Seems to me when the dog started barking it was after one. Just about exactly a quarter after.

ALICE: [*Flustered. Pinning her hope on bravado*] Gee, Pop, you've got good ears, haven't you? I thought your door was closed.

POP: It was. Where my daughter's welfare is concerned, I have very good ears. What I'd like to stress, young lady, is that after that I heard you and George rattling dishes in the kitchen. And giggling away.

ALICE: [*Weakly*] Oh, Pop.

BILLY: What was so funny, Alice? The political situation? [POP *glares at* BILLY. MOM *enters with tray, quickly clears rest of dishes, exits R.*]

POP: Please realize why I'm bringing up this matter. It's not only you I'm thinking about—there's George. First off, you're ruining that young man's career. I hear he has a good job. Well, if he wants to be fresh in the morning, he's got to have sleep. [*Warming up, flourishing arm*] You want him to succeed, don't you? How can he climb to the top if he gallivants with you till all hours of the night?

ALICE: But it was a Friday night, Pop. George's place is closed Saturdays.

POP: [*More irritated, raising voice*] When I was his age, I never kept a high-school senior up past midnight. I had more sense. And more respect for her!

ALICE: But times have changed——

MOM: [*Appearing at kitchen door, dish towel in hand*] Daddy, Daddy—dear, not so loud.

POP: Okay, Amy.

MOM: The Brysons' windows are open. They can hear every word. [*Disappears L.*]

POP: [*Lower*] Well, I'm sure Mr. Bryson would agree with me. Matter of fact, he took in the same lecture I did at the P.T.A. last week. By that professor with the long chin. And who made me go to that meeting, anyway? [*Glowers at* ALICE.]

ALICE: [*In self-defense*] You know every father's expected to attend—at least twice a year.

POP: [*Louder again*] Don't change the subject! What I want to point out, young lady, is what I distinctly heard the speaker say. He repeated it over and over. It's our duty as parents to lay down clear—clear!—firm rules for our children! Let them know what we expect of them! He said, "Don't be unpredictable, just set up standards. Work them out ahead of time. Have them definitely understood. By everyone!" [*Banging fist on table*] Well, I'm making a rule. I won't have you staying out so late any more. Twelve o'clock is your curfew. [*Banging*] Twelve o'clock!

MOM: [*Reappearing at kitchen door*] Take it easy, Dad. That was a heavy meal.

POP: All right, Mom. [MOM *disappears L.*] Maybe I ought to write out "12 o'clock" and have you sign it. He said that, too. Said some families set the rules down on paper and every member signs it!

ALICE: Yes, but didn't he also say to change the rules as your kids mature?

POP: I'll notify you when there's a change! [*Kindly*] I don't want to upset you, kiddy. I like you to have a good time. [*Folding napkin*] Every father does. But we know what's best.

ALICE: [*Upset*] Gee, Pop, you're—you're old-fashioned! You don't understand!

POP: Oh, yes, I do.

ALICE: It isn't as though we were just wandering around somewhere. George always takes me to such wonderful places. We couldn't go anywhere if I had to be home by midnight.

POP: [*Decisively*] While you're living under my roof you'll obey my rules. Why, these late hours'll affect your grades before you know it. I want every young man who calls here told the rules. *Especially* George!

BILLY: [*Teasing*] Say, Alice, is George in love with you? Has he told you yet?

ALICE: [*Rising, irate*] Billy Mygatt! Pop, make him get out!

POP: [*Paternally perverse*] What's the matter? Anything you're embarrassed to have him hear?

ALICE: Of course not! [*Sits again.*]

BILLY: Say, Alice, where'd you go last night, anyway?

ALICE: If you must know, Mr. B.—short for brat, not Billy—we went to a night club where George knows the band leader.

BILLY: [*Chirping*] But does the band leader know George?

ALICE: That's the last time I tell you anything!

POP: [*Sharply*] That's enough! I hope I've made myself clear, Alice. You're not staying out past twelve any more. That's my rule! . . . Now, do we understand each other?

ALICE: [*Tearfully*] Someone would think I was a child!

POP: [*Raising voice again*] Now don't start crying! It won't help! [ALICE *wipes eyes with handkerchief.* BILLY *sneaks a grin which* POP *catches.*] What's so funny, young man? You may leave the room!

BILLY: [*Subdued*] Yes, sir. [*Shuffles out U.R.C.*]

POP: The very next time George sets foot in this house I want to have a heart-to-heart talk with him! I'll let him know who gives the orders around here! I'll teach him a thing or two! I'll tell him off!

MOM: [*Entering from kitchen*] Daddy, I wish you'd control yourself. The Brysons may have visitors.

POP: [*Annoyed but modulating*] All right, Amy. But this is my house. [MOM *removes napkins, tablecloth and pad, then exits to kitchen.*]

BILLY: [*Peeking in U.R.C.*] Can I come in to get my paper?

POP: [*Emphatically*] No! NO!

BILLY: [*Ducking out of sight*] Yes, sir.

POP: As a matter of fact, young lady, I've just decided there'll be no dates for you this week end. That's so you can catch up on sleep!

ALICE: [*In protest*] But, Pop!

POP: What?

ALICE: I have a date tonight. In a little while.

POP: Oh, you have?

ALICE: Uh-huh.

POP: And who's calling for you tonight?

ALICE: [*Tiny voice*] George.

POP: What again? You can't go!

ALICE: But it's a special concert. Jiminy, can't I even go to a concert?

POP: Never mind! [*Rises and paces.*] So! George Hollingshead is calling for you here? Tonight?

ALICE: [*Quaking*] Yes.

POP: [*Lustily*] Well! Well, well! When I get finished with him he'll be giving a concert. A grand concert! No—wait—I'll lead the band! I'll trumpet at him! I'll make his ears vibrate! [BILLY *peeks in U.R.C.*] He'll know he can't come around here ruining the health of a growing girl. He'll learn you can't go out tonight! [*Stalks out U.R.C., narrowly avoiding collision with* BILLY.]

BILLY: Oops, sorry. Like a subway rush, hey, Dad? [POP *disappears R. Retrieving paper*] Pop's on the warpath, all right. Must have had a bad day at the office.

ALICE: Well, you certainly aren't any help.

BILLY: Oh, I don't know. I could have told Pop I'd wear a big 12 on my baseball uniform. But I didn't, did I? Hey, why don't you phone George and call off the date? Then Pop'll calm down 'n' everything'll be hunky-dory.

ALICE: Good idea, Billy—but I can't use it. George has to do some research at a library, and he's coming over from there. Anyway, he's on his way.

MOM: [*Entering with unsorted silverware*] Billy, the grocer is saving rolls for me and I forgot to call for them. Run around the corner please, honey.

BILLY: [*Lugubriously*] Do I have to go now, Mom?

MOM: They'll close soon, Billy. Better scoot.

BILLY: Okay. Hope I don't miss anything! [*Exits U.R.C.* MOM *and* ALICE *sort silverware into buffet drawer.*]

ALICE: [*Greatly distressed*] Oh, Mom, what'll I do? Did you hear Pop's rules and things? And to top it all, he's planning to insult George. I—I'll die!

MOM: Now, honey, Dad has a lot on his mind. And worrying about you, too—well, he loses his temper. But there's a good deal of right on his side. Don't forget that.

ALICE: Yes, Mom. I know I'm out late sometimes—but, gee, not during the school week when it really matters.

MOM: [*Patiently*] We've discussed this all before, dear.

ALICE: But I can't be a spoilsport. I can't keep telling my date I want to go home!

MOM: Well, when you start out, tell him your curfew. Then it's his place to get you here on time.

ALICE: But what if there's a long show, or a whole crowd to take home . . . ?

MOM: [*Firmly*] You can still get home by a reasonable hour.

ALICE: Oh, Mom, will Dad say something awful to George?

MOM: [*Dryly*] I've learned never to predict what a man will do. Of course, I know your father pretty well . . . I haven't just walked around the block with him. He wants above all to do what's right for his children. Sometimes he carries out his threats to the hilt. Once in a while he's more sizzle than pop.

ALICE: This time he's *really* angry!

MOM: Well, this rumpus has been some time a-comin', dear. You've given him cause to. . . .

ALICE: But if he goes ahead, George'll think I'm just a baby. Why, nowadays. . . .

POP: [*Appearing U.R.C.*] Where's this George Hollingshead? What's keeping him?

ALICE: [*Wistfully*] He'd've phoned if he couldn't come.

POP: Well, I'll be waiting for him! [*Disappears.*]

ALICE: [*Moaning*] Ohh. I'll never be able to look George in the face again. I *know* it!

MOM: [*Comfortingly*] The world's not going to end, dear.

ALICE: [*Wailing*] Oh, Mom!

MOM: If George is as fine as you think, things'll work out some- how.

ALICE: They always do, but not—not always the way you want them.

POP: [*Off, roaring*] I don't like to be kept waiting!

MOM: Oh, dear, your father's very upset! [*Exits L. to kitchen.*]

ALICE: [*Trails her to door.*] I suppose there's no use going up to change. And I was planning to wear my new dress tonight, too. [*Sits disconsolately at table.*]

BILLY: [*Hastening in U.R.C. with paper bag*] What gives? Any new developments? [ALICE *shakes her head feebly. Exiting L.*] Here're the rolls, Mom. They were just gonna sell 'em. [*Returns, sits and picks up newspaper.*] Woww! Catch this, Alice? "Enraged Father Thrashes Daughter's Suitor." Some headline writer I am, hey?

ALICE: Billy Mygatt, you ought to be on my side. Your day will come.

BILLY: [*Blithely*] I'm a boy. [*The telephone rings.* ALICE *hurries to answer.* POP *appears in doorway U.R.C.*] If that's for me, Miss Mygatt, I'm in conference.

ALICE: [*Into phone, nervously*] Hello. Yes. Just a minute, please. [*Calling*] Billy. [POP *disappears U.R.C.*]

BILLY: [*Crosses. Into phone*] Hello? H'ya. What's cookin'? Uh-huh. Uh-huh. No. I don't want to come over now. No, he didn't say I've gotta stay in. No, Mom isn't sore at me. Can't tell you why right now. See you at Sunday school. Bring your catcher's mitt. Well, maybe I'll make it later. It depends. So long, Spike. [*Hangs up, returns to table.*] Aw, nuts, that wasn't Spike. It was Spud.

ALICE: Your life's awfully complicated, isn't it?

BILLY: Oh, can't compare with some people's. [*Turns on radio, gets dance band.*]

ALICE: Shut that thing off, will you? [BILLY *turns radio off.*]

POP: [*Entering U.R.C.*] If you've finished memorizing the sport section, I'd like the newspaper.

BILLY: Sure, Pop, sure. Here it is. [POP *sits, rises and turns on the radio. The same band is playing.* POP *lowers volume, settles down and opens the paper.*]

MOM: [*Appearing L.*] Wouldn't you be more comfortable in the living room, Dad?

POP: What I have to do doesn't involve comfort. I'm not going to budge from this spot till he comes. Alice, when that George fellow arrives, send him in here.

ALICE: [*Glumly*] Yes, Dad.

MOM: But the living room's so much pleasanter for company. . . .

POP: Amy, this is one affair I'm managing myself! [*Slaps table.*]

MOM: Whatever you say, dear. [*Disappears L.*]

BILLY: How about a game of chess, Pop? [POP *glares at* BILLY.] Okay, okay, I was only asking. How about you, Alice?

ALICE: Billy, will you pul-*lease* go and get lost?

POP: [*Barking*] A little quiet here, children!

BILLY: [*Loud whisper*] Say, Alice, do you think George is standing you up? [ALICE, *annoyed, gestures "Be quiet!" The doorbell rings. There is a tense silence.*]

POP: Aha! There he is! [*Drops paper, rises.*] Alice, aren't you going to the door?

ALICE: [*Meekly*] Yes, Dad. [*Leaves U.R.C.* POP *straightens his tie, fusses with cuffs, clears his throat. Off*] Come in here, George. [ALICE *and* GEORGE *enter U.R.C.*]

GEORGE: [*Well-poised, genially*] Good evening, everybody. How's the Mygatt family tonight?

POP: [*Austerely*] Very well, young man.

MOM: [*Peeking in from L.*] Good evening, George.

GEORGE: Hello there, Mrs. Mygatt. How have you been?

MOM: Just fine.

GEORGE: You're looking mighty well this evening.

MOM: Thank you, George. [*Disappears L.*]

BILLY: That's some tie, George! [*Clicks tongue.*]

GEORGE: [*Pleasantly*] So you like knitted ones, too? [*Loud whisper*] I'll tell you a secret, Bill. They're my weakness!

BILLY: I'll remind Alice before Christmas.

ALICE: [*Weakly*] If you'll excuse me. . . .

GEORGE: Sure! [*Embarrassed,* ALICE *wheels and hastens off L.*] Isn't that Webb Johnson's orchestra? [POP *flicks off radio.*] Your ear's very discriminating, Mr. Mygatt. Johnson's outfit isn't what it used to be. [POP *blows his nose.*]

POP: [*Determinedly*] Young man, I want to have a word with you. There happens to be something very definite I have in mind. Yes, indeed. As a matter of fact, might interest you to know I've just told Alice—uh—I have—[*Sharply*] Billy!

BILLY: Yes, Pop?

POP: Seems to me you have homework to attend to.

BILLY: Only one book to read and that's a snap.

POP: [*Sternly*] Well, leave the room, anyway.

BILLY: Yes, sir. [*Exits U.R.C.*]

GEORGE: A fine, bright youngster—that boy of yours.

POP: [*Wryly*] Thank you.

GEORGE: Shows a good home behind him. Alice, of course, is proof of that, too.

POP: [*Ominously*] Sit down, young man. [POP *blows his nose.*] Glad we have some privacy. [GEORGE *sits, studying* POP. POP *moves around the table, vaguely straightening chairs.*] Young man, I've been waiting to let you know exactly how I feel about your going out with Alice. Er—um—as a matter of fact—uh—well, it seems to me it's about time you know where I stand. I believe it's best to state the thing flatly. I am of the opinion. . . .

GEORGE: [*Interrupting, with an affable, confiding air*] Excuse me, sir. I'd like to offer my apologies for being late. You see, I'm working on a special report for my *supervisor*. And—well, sir, I'm afraid I just lost track of time. [*Lowering voice*] That report might bring me a promotion, you know. But don't mention it to Alice. I want it to be a surprise.

POP: [*Grimly*] I won't.

GEORGE: Pretty important research I'm doing. I've stumbled on a few original angles.

POP: [*Perfunctorily*] That's interesting—glad to hear it. [POP *moves uncertainly to radio, flicks it on and off.* MOM, *wiping a dish, appears at kitchen door and eavesdrops.*] To get back to what I was saying. I was telling my wife and Alice about a speaker on juvenile delinquency I heard at P.T.A. He said the way to——

GEORGE: [*Quickly*] Oh, that world-famous psychologist?

POP: That's the man.

GEORGE: He has a splendid reputation, sir. You must have enjoyed him tremendously.

POP: Well—I did, on the whole.

GEORGE: Good!

POP: The man had some theories I'd like to see put into practice right in this house. Consequently . . . I've just made a rule about the time Alice has to be home——

GEORGE: [*Heartily*] Mr. Mygatt, you're a man to be admired. Not many fathers come away from a lecture and put into practice what they hear from an authority——

POP: What's more—I have every intention of sticking to it.

GEORGE: That's very wise, sir.

POP: Now when you see Alice this evening, she'll make it clear to you, too. She knows exactly how I feel.

MOM: [*Calling suddenly*] All right, Alice! Bring in the tray, dear. [GEORGE *rises. Wearing an apron,* ALICE *enters L. with pie, milk, coffee, cream, sugar.*] George, I want you to taste this pie. I thought Billy'd never stop eating it! [ALICE *sets tray on table.*] There's a big cup of coffee for you, Daddy. You look as if you'd like one. [*Serves* GEORGE *pie and milk.*]

GEORGE: [*Sitting*] Mmm! Apricot, my favorite!

MOM: It's peach, George.

GEORGE: Looks elegant, anyway, Mrs. Mygatt.

MOM: Thank you, George.

GEORGE: [*Helpfully*] How much sugar, sir? Would you like cream?

POP: [*Grimly*] I'll drink it black. [*Takes cup, sets it on buffet.* GEORGE *eats.*]

MOM: [*Lightly*] We had a pleasant surprise. Billy bought rolls at the grocer and in the bag was a plastic cake knife. A souvenir for their anniversary. Now wasn't that nice, Dad?

POP: [*Gruffly*] Yes, Amy.

MOM: Oh, Alice. Freshen up, dear—just in case Dad decides you can go out tonight. There isn't time to change.

ALICE: [*Gulping*] Yes, Mom. [POP *gives no sign.* ALICE *hastens out U.R.C.*]

MOM: My, the weather's been so erratic. Did it look like rain when you came, George?

GEORGE: I didn't notice, Mrs. Mygatt. Want me to look out?

POP: [*Sourly*] The paper said fair and warmer.

MOM: Good. The sun always makes things more cheerful.

GEORGE: You're so right, Mrs. Mygatt.

POP: [*Clearing throat*] Hruh! Amy——

MOM: Oh, have I interrupted you two? Maybe I'd better clean the roasting pan.

GEORGE: Thanks a hundred for the snack.

MOM: You're quite welcome, George. [*Exits L.* GEORGE *finishes pie and milk.*]

GEORGE: Your wife's a mighty good baker, sir. [*Looks at wrist watch.*] Tch! Why does it take a woman so long to get ready?

BILLY: [*Appearing U.R.C.*] Can I come in yet, Pop?

POP: No.

BILLY: But I left my baseball guide on the buffet.

POP: I thought you had a book to read.

BILLY: Aw, I know what happens. I read the last chapter.

POP: Well, go back and read the middle.

BILLY: If you insist. [*Exits U.R.C.*]

GEORGE: [*Reaching into pocket*] Like a peppermint, sir?

POP: [*Brusquely*] No thanks.

GEORGE: [*Taking candy*] Cigarette?

POP: No thank you.

GEORGE: Oh, that's right—you're cigars. I know a special brand you might like——

POP: [*Bracing himself anew*] To get back to the subject, George —uh—I've been meaning to suggest—er—tell you . . . what I've been wanting to get at is this:

GEORGE: [*Earnestly*] If there's anything I can do for you, sir, don't hesitate to mention it!

POP: Well, as I've been telling Alice, there has to be a definite time that everyone knows about—and there shouldn't be any doubt in anyone's mind——

ALICE: [*Appears U.R.C. with handbag and gloves. Uncertainly*] Daddy, I'm ready—if you say I can go. [GEORGE *rises.*] We'll miss the beginning if we don't leave right away. Okay, Pop . . . huh?

POP: [*Clears throat. Roaring*] Oh, you're ready? [ALICE *nods timidly.*]

GEORGE: Hate to walk out on you, sir. It's been wonderful to have a chat. But it *is* getting late.

POP: Well. . . . Well. . . . Go on, you two! Clear out! What are you waiting for? [ALICE *blows* POP *a kiss gratefully.*]

GEORGE: Right you are. Thanks for giving me some of your time, Mr. Mygatt. Good night. [*Calling*] Good night, Mom.

MOM: [*Appearing L.*] Good night, children. Hope you enjoy yourselves.

GEORGE: Oh, we will. Thanks again for the pie. [*Moves U.R.C., takes* ALICE'S *arm.*]

POP: What time do you people plan to be home?

GEORGE: [*Genially*] Oh, somewhere around one.

POP: [*Gruffly*] Try to keep it closer to twelve.

ALICE: [*Quickly*] We'll really try, Dad. We'd better hurry, George! [GEORGE *and* ALICE *exeunt U.R.C.* POP *moves to door U.R.C., clasps his hands behind his back, and frowns after them.*]

BILLY: [*Entering U.R.C*] How'd you score that one, Pop? Win, lose, or draw?

POP: [*Sternly*] Never mind, young man. Where are *you* going?

BILLY: [*Taking baseball guide*] Over to Spud Jarrell's. He has to mind his kid sister. [*Exiting U.R.C.*] Good night, Pop.

POP: [*Calling after him*] Well, you get in early. And I don't want any two ways about it! Hear me? *Early!* [*Sighs, flicks on radio, flicks it off, lights cigar, puffs, chomps. Calling into kitchen*] Amy! Did you punish the dog for running out without a muzzle?

MOM: [*Off L.*] Yes, dear.

POP: [*Flatly*] That George What's-his-name has a good head on his shoulders. Seems pretty intelligent. [*Blows nose, moves U.R.C. Reflecting*] Do you think he was fencing with me? [*Vigorously*] No—guess he knew better than to try! And anyway, you can bet your bottom dollar I'll tell him off if they're home later than one! I'll come out in my bathrobe and my slippers! So help me!

MOM: [*Entering L.*] You're very right, dear. [POP *exits U.R.C.* MOM *smiles and places cup on tray. Tolerantly*] Just the way my dad used to be. More sizzle than pop!

The Curtain Falls.

NOTES ON STAGING

DATE-TIME is a family comedy notably easy to act and stage. It's comfortably short. And it appeals to all age levels, entertaining teen-agers, parents, grandparents, young fry, and bachelor uncles. Note the small cast. A boon to many groups!

Acting

POP, MOM, ALICE, and BILLY MYGATT should come across the footlights as a close-knit family. They know each other from way back when.

Dessert is about over when *Date-Time* begins. But there is a limited amount of eating. Introduce real food at rehearsals so actors won't pick up cues with mouths jammed.

ALICE copes with POP'S displeasure with dignity—and deep anguish. MOM, the diplomat, walks a tightrope, supporting POP, sympathetic to ALICE.

POP ought to become familiar at rehearsals with the brand of cigar the property man will supply. One unprepared POP literally stopped the show when he lit up the stogy a bargain-hunting prop man had stashed in his pocket! Incidentally, omit the smoking if it's in any way objectionable.

There is leeway in casting almost-teen BILLY. He can be played by someone older, boy or girl—who will convey the part by walking, standing, and gesturing with gawky, fidgety, controlled high spirit. Loose, slightly outgrown clothes and a voice pitched a bit high will help the impression. If you have an actor younger than twelve, he will fit too.

GEORGE HOLLINGSHEAD should act suave and self-assured, but likably so. He seems relaxed—yet is in command!

Scenery and Furnishings

Date-Time's dining room can range from simple to lavish. Your budget and resources decide.

A dining room can be suggested readily. Stage directions call for a few specific furnishings. Lacking them, borrow from a home or store. Fill in details but avoid clutter. Wanted: a room *as a whole* that is a warm, attractive background for the MYGATTS.

Fashioning the room's physical confines—its walls and doors—depends again on resources. The Guide advises on using flats, drapes, and screens. (By the way, the scenery for *She Loves Him Yes* is very similar.)

Notice that both doors can remain open through the play. If your carpentry is shaky, there need be no slamming to pull the scenery down! (You might like to substitute an archway for the door U.R.C.)

Do not overlook backing for doorways if sight lines permit peeking through. You can also place strategically a table and vase, lamp, chair, picture, etc., to suggest more of the house.

Properties

Prominent on the prop list is a pie. Possibly a bakery, welcoming publicity and plural gratitude, will donate samples. Otherwise induce a mother or group member to provide one for each performance. Give program credit.

Borrow the telephone from the local company office. Advance notice is generally needed.

Costumes and Make-up

The garb of a moderate-income family suits the play. Clothe ALICE in dominant, clear colors. This heightens her youth and vivacity. Her accessories ought to complement her dress.

Clothe MOM more conservatively. And POP is no fashion plate.

BILLY is something of a faddist and sports fan. What are the pre-teen clothing rages in town? Adopt stageworthy ones for him.

GEORGE deserves well-fitting, stylish clothes. He must feel he looks topnotch. Do not forget his knitted tie.

POP and MOM need middle-age make-up. Apply in moderation, though, for they are only fortyish. Check the pat-by-pat treatment of make-up in the Guide.

Special Effects and Lighting

Radio, telephone, and doorbell are the sound man's concern. For the radio, play a nonvocal record off stage. For the bells, there are many alternatives listed under Special Effects in the Guide.

No specific light changes are called for in the script.

Publicity

Remember this play's appeal to a span of age levels. It concerns a problem that is familiar to practically every family.

Date-Time has been performed in the United States, Canada, and the Philippines. You can truthfully claim international success for it. Advertise wisely (see Guide), and fill your theater!

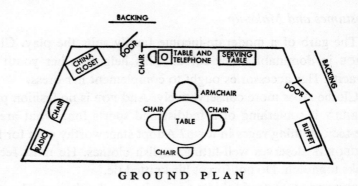

GROUND PLAN

FURNISHINGS	PROPERTIES	
radio	baseball guide	cigar
china closet	telephone	newspaper
buffet	tablecloth and pad	apron
telephone table	dessert dishes	dish towel
serving table	cups	handkerchiefs for
dining table	pie	ALICE, POP
armchair	fruit bowl with	filled paper bag
chairs	pears, apples, etc.	glass of milk
	tray	cream pitcher
	napkins	sugar bowl
	silverware	peppermints

Dooley and the Amateur Hour

A ONE-ACT COMEDY*
BY EDWIN & NATHALIE GROSS

Cast of Characters

JACK DOOLEY	chipper, self-confident, likable, part-time doorman at the Taj Mahal Theater. In his late teens.
PEGGY CAMPBELL	pretty, level-headed, part-time cashier at the Taj Mahal Theater. In her late teens.
MRS. BURNSIDE	bossy but kindly. The theater manager.
KITTY PARKER	designing, affected, well-dressed. In her late teens.
RAYMOND PARKER	Kitty's younger brother, who thinks he can sing.
HERMAN WICZYNSKI	a football hero, husky, overbearing, and not too bright. In his late teens.
GLADYS WICZYNSKI	Herman's sister, who plays the violin. (*Note:* another musical instrument may be substituted.)
MRS. STEIG	a pushing mother.

*Adapted from a *Seventeen* magazine story by Charles Alden Peterson.

ERMINTRUDE STEIG   her bashful daughter, who can sing.

TWO JUDGES

PERFORMERS FROM YOUR GROUP

PLACE: The lobby and stage of the Taj Mahal Theater.

TIME: Saturday afternoon. Before, during, and after Amateur Hour.

PART I

The curtain rises on the inner lobby of the Taj Mahal Theater. It is fairly bare. Billboards along the walls advertise moving pictures. Up center stands a large sign reading: "Taj Mahal Theater Introducing Amateur Hour Today! Prizes!!!" The sign blocks the ticket box and doorway leading to the theater proper. A door up left center says "Manager's Office" and one at stage left says "Emergency Exit." The door leading off to the cashier's booth and street is down right.

PEGGY CAMPBELL *enters down right. She stops before a billboard, studies it, mimics the languid pose of the heroine, and grins. She starts to move the "Amateur Hour" sign but has some difficulty lifting it. Whistling jauntily,* JACK DOOLEY *saunters in from the street. He wears a doorman's uniform.*

DOOLEY: Afternoon, Peggy. Wait—that's a job for two. Move over.

PEGGY: Thanks, Dooley. [*They carry sign R.*]

DOOLEY: Amateurs today! Goody, goody-goody! Everyone pours into this palace of the cinema at once, and no work for Dooley while the show is on. [*Assumed basso voice*] Step right up! Have your tickets ready! Plenty of seats for all.

Balcony through the door and to your left. No shoving, pul-lease! [*Barking*] Hey, you—how old are you? [*Falsetto*] Four on the train, five for real, and six in school. [*Basso*] Don't you know you have to be with an adult? Madam, would you mind keeping an eye on this little boy? [*Tittering falsetto*] Oh, my no. Isn't he sweet? Come, sonny. [*Basso*] Much obliged, Madam.

PEGGY: [*Sincerely*] You're a wonderful doorman, Dooley.

DOOLEY: [*Blithely*] You're a wonderful cashier, Peggy.

PEGGY: [*Curtseying*] Thank you, sir.

DOOLEY: [*Bowing*] Thank you. If I ever get out of school, I have a profession. Tell me, how serious are you about being a cashier?

PEGGY: As serious as you about being a doorman, Dooley.

DOOLEY: Good—we're both in this for the laughs. And the money. My father has the weirdest ideas about allowances.

PEGGY: Mine, too. [*Sighs.*]

DOOLEY: Not that the pay here is stupendous. I've been thinking of asking for a raise—[MRS. BURNSIDE *enters from the manager's office. Two strips of adhesive tape adorn her forehead.*] Afternoon, Mrs. Burnside. Lovely day for the Taj Mahal's first try with an amateur hour.

MRS. BURNSIDE: That's right, Dooley. [*Soberly*] I want to talk to you.

PEGGY: Then you'll excuse me. Is the money ready?

MRS. BURNSIDE: Yes, Peg. On my desk. [PEGGY *exits U.L.C. With contained anger*] Jack Dooley. I didn't blow up when you fixed the water fountain—and caused a flood. I held my temper when you went to work on the popcorn machine—

and it cost me eighteen dollars. But *what* is that gimmick you installed in the projection booth?

DOOLEY: [*Relieved*] Oh, that! I put up a few of them yesterday. Now you can relax, Mrs. Burnside. That's a burglar trap.

MRS. BURNSIDE: [*Grimly*] Oh.

DOOLEY: It'd make a whale of a racket if someone tripped it.

MRS. BURNSIDE: [*Fingering tape*] It did.

DOOLEY: Holy smokes, ma'am! You mean . . . ?

MRS. BURNSIDE: If that trap had fallen any harder, they'd be holding the post-mortem right now.

DOOLEY: [*Smiling wryly*] Well, that shows the thing works, anyway.

MRS. BURNSIDE: Dooley. I'm flirting with oblivion keeping you on the payroll. Someday you'll wire dynamite to the safe, forgetting I'm the one who opens it.

DOOLEY: [*Alarmed*] Mrs. Burnside! You're not firing me?

MRS. BURNSIDE: [*Threateningly*] I'm not? [*Pause*] No. Guess I'm not. I need you today, Dooley.

DOOLEY: [*Relieved*] Good. Always ready to serve.

MRS. BURNSIDE: You're going to be master of ceremonies for the Amateur Hour.

DOOLEY: Wha-a-t?

MRS. BURNSIDE: The man from the radio station can't make it. And I'm counting on this show to help business. So I'm not going to call it off. You're comedian enough.

DOOLEY: [*Protestingly*] But—but Mrs. Burnside, I—I'm— [*Cagily*] Do I get fired if I don't do it?

MRS. BURNSIDE: You'll do it, Dooley. You know the patter. There'll be two judges besides you. Your main job will be announcing the numbers.

DOOLEY: [*Weakly*] But Mrs. Burnside——

MRS. BURNSIDE: And I don't believe in stage fright, Mr. Emcee. See you later. [*Exits to street.*]

DOOLEY: [*Wailing*] Ooooh! [*Louder*] Oooohh! [PEGGY *enters from manager's office with small money bag.*]

PEGGY: Jack Dooley, are you sick?

DOOLEY: If I'm not I ought to be. Right now I place this 360th of all my days in the year. Mrs. Burnside said I have to emcee the Amateur Hour.

PEGGY: [*Pleased*] Why, Dooley, what a break!

DOOLEY: Traitor! Can you picture me up on the stage with a bunch of—of amateurs?

PEGGY: Of course. You'll love it.

DOOLEY: They'll hog the spotlight—and swarm all over me! Then they'll all want prizes, and there's no telling—[KITTY PARKER *enters from the street. She is trailed by* RAYMOND *wearing a cowboy outfit including a lariat, chaps, spurs, cuffs, sombrero, boots, scarf, holsters, and brilliant shirt. Happily*] Kitty!

KITTY: [*Affected*] Hello, Jackie. You'll pardon us, won't you, Peggy?

PEGGY: Why, yes. I was just leaving. [*Exchanges stiff smiles with* KITTY *and exits D.R.*]

KITTY: [*Unctuously*] I'm so glad to see you, Dooley. [*Pouting sweetly*] You haven't been around all week.

DOOLEY: [*Devotedly*] I know. I wanted to see you—but I've been up to my clavicle in Bio.

KITTY: It must be simply too enervating.

DOOLEY: I'll call you the first minute I'm free. [*Lowering voice*] Say, it's a little early to let you into the show for nothing.

KITTY: Oh, Jackie, that's not what I want—today. My brother Raymond's going to be one of the amateurs.

DOOLEY: [*Sharply*] What's that?

KITTY: Yes. He was notified this morning.

RAYMOND: Sure thing. [*Condescendingly*] Hi, chum.

DOOLEY: [*Sourly*] Hello, pard.

KITTY: He's going to sing "Oh, Bury Me Not on the Lone Prairie." And he's frabjous! We just bought his costume. Aren't you thrilled?

DOOLEY: [*Same*] Thrilled to pieces.

KITTY: I knew you would be. Raymond, wait for Big Sis outside.

RAYMOND: Aw, Kitty, you're always making me——

KITTY: [*Snapping*] Raymond Parker! [RAYMOND *ambles out D.R. Wheedling*] Jackie, I—I don't imagine there's any question about first prize, is there?

DOOLEY: Oh, no. It's fifteen dollars, all right.

KITTY: That isn't what I mean. It's not the money, it's—oh, Jackie, I'd be so happy if Raymond won! After all, these things are only a matter of opinion. Of course I wouldn't ask you to do anything dishonest, and I know you're not in charge or anything, but if you could just use your influence with the judges? [*Slipping arms around his neck*] Do you suppose you could?

DOOLEY: Well——

KITTY: For me?

DOOLEY: [*Miserably*] I su-suppose, Kitty. Maybe.

KITTY: You mean you *will*?

DOOLEY: [*Overwhelmed, gasping*] Ah—probably.

KITTY: Jackie, darling, I knew I could count on you! And you can count on me for the Senior Prom! [*Plants quick kiss on cheek.*] 'Bye now, angel! [*Skitters out D.R.* DOOLEY *is woebegone. He stands thinking, then slowly starts U.C.* HERMAN WICZYNSKI *struts in from the street. He wears a football letter sweater. He crosses to* DOOLEY *and whacks him on the back.*]

HERMAN: [*Booming*] Hiya, Jack!

DOOLEY: [*Unenthusiastically, rubbing shoulder*] Oh, hello, Herman.

HERMAN: Jack, ol' pal, ol' pal, the girl out front—er, Peg Campbell I think it is—tells me you got yourself a job emceeing this amateur show today.

DOOLEY: That's right.

HERMAN: Dandy! You're just the man I want to see. Do you like violins?

DOOLEY: Well, I can take 'em or leave 'em alone. Why?

HERMAN: My sister Gladys is a champ on the violin. And she's entered in your contest.

DOOLEY: That's nice.

Dooley and the Amateur Hour • 1 3 3

HERMAN: This is stric'ly confidential. The whole Wiczynski family's excited. My kid brother who's ten pounds heavier than me—my big brother who's the State weight-liftin' marvel—and my pop who can lick the three of us—we're all expectin' Gladdy to cop first prize.

DOOLEY: Lot of other folks want it, too.

HERMAN: True. That's what makes it so difficult. You see, Jack, Gladys is such a sensitive, high-strung girl.

DOOLEY: Oh.

HERMAN: She bruises easy, and I don't want her to get hurt. I can see her now—stumblin' home with her violin under one arm, weepin' her heart out 'cause she didn't win. [*Indignantly*] Buddy, you know, if that happened all us Wiczynskis might fly off the handle and start beatin' people up! On second thought [*Feeling* DOOLEY'S *upper arm*] maybe I can take on the job myself.

DOOLEY: [*Gulping*] I get your point.

HERMAN: I thought you would! And *don't* forget it! Gladys Wiczynski! See you around, Jack, ol' pal. [*Feints at* DOOLEY *and shadowboxes out D.R.*]

PEGGY: [*Appears D.R. Calling*] They're lining up outside, Dooley. I'm opening the box office soon.

DOOLEY: [*Weakly*] Peggy, I'm in trouble.

PEGGY: [*Crossing*] What's wrong?

DOOLEY: That overgrown football hero has a sister with a violin. And if she doesn't win first prize I get massacred. By every Wiczynski in town.

PEGGY: Pooh! I know the whole family and they're all good sports. They wouldn't gang up on you.

DOOLEY: [*Sickly*] I'm beginning to feel the spot behind the eight-ball is my home away from home.

PEGGY: I'll bet the whole thing is Herman's idea.

DOOLEY: Herman can gang up on me all by himself, remember. And then I practic'ly promised Kitty Parker—er—um—never mind. Where's Mrs. Burnside? I'll just resign right now.

PEGGY: Jack Dooley. You'll go out on that stage and do the best you can. I'll help!

DOOLEY: [*Doggedly*] Well, I won't run a contest that's not on the level.

PEGGY: Why shouldn't it be on the level? What are you? A man or a mouse?

DOOLEY: [*Squeaking*] A man. [*Firmly*] A man!

The Curtain Falls.

PART II

The stage of the Taj Mahal Theater a short time later. The scene is played in front of the curtain. MRS. BURNSIDE *enters left, carries a microphone center.*

MRS. BURNSIDE: Good afternoon, everyone. It's a pleasure to welcome you to the Taj Mahal Theater's first Amateur Hour. I hope you'll enjoy it. Jack Dooley is the man of the hour. He has kindly volunteered to fill in as master of ceremonies. Many of you know him, so we'll omit further introduction. Come on out, Dooley. Let's give him a hearty welcome! [*Leads applause.* DOOLEY *enters L. in his doorman's uniform minus cap.* NOTE: *throughout the ensuing scene responses of applause and laughter are ensured by members of cast seated in the audience.*]

DOOLEY: [*With stage presence but slightly nervous*] Thanks, Mrs. Burnside. Hello, everybody. [MRS. BURNSIDE *exits L.*] I didn't exactly expect to find myself emceeing today, so just count me in as one of the amateurs. Too bad I'm not eligible for one of the prizes. [*Smacking hands*] Well, this should be an interesting job. My father always said I wasn't afraid of work—I'd lie down right beside it and go to sleep. I'd feel a lot better with a joke book in my pocket. You know—one of those things that says, "Question: How do you make a Venetian blind? Answer: Stick a finger in his eye." Anyway, folks, when I look into your faces—and believe me, your faces need looking into—oops, better stick to business. Let's sail into the details of this contest. First prize will be a great big unbounceable check of fifteen dollars. And all our other competitors will get three double-passes to the Taj Mahal. Let's see—I have one here. This small print says, [*Reading*] "Not good Saturdays, Sundays, Holidays,"—well, never mind. Now for the judging. There are three judges in all. Two of them are sitting down there with you in the audience. I won't tell you who they are till the show's over, but take my word for it, they know talent! I'm the third judge. Of course—uh—I add up to a minority. I hardly count. Oh, yes. Your applause, ladies and gentlemen, will make the performers feel good. It will also help the judges. Their decision will be final. Just a second, please. [*Exits L. and returns with* PEGGY. *Each carries a chair and sets it D.L.*] I want you to meet Peggy Campbell. She's a lot cuter to look at than I am. She'll help me out up here. So how about a hand for Peg? [*Applause.* PEGGY *waves.*] Now to start off the parade of stars, folks, we have . . . [*Consulting list*] Miss Ermintrude Steig! [*Leads applause.* ERMINTRUDE *and* MRS. STEIG *come down the aisle from seats in audience.* PEGGY *helps them mount the stage.*] Ahh! *Two* lovely ladies! Which is who?

MRS. STEIG: I'm Ermintrude's mother.

DOOLEY: Ah, here we have Ermintrude and Mrs. Steig. Or shall we say Ermintrude and her inspiration? [MRS. STEIG *simpers.*] Wait over there please, Mrs. Steig. [MRS. STEIG *moves L.*] A chair for the lady, Peg. Well, Ermintrude, what have you decided to do for us? [ERMINTRUDE *hangs head shyly.*]

MRS. STEIG: [*Calling*] She's going to sing.

DOOLEY: Good! And what are you going to sing?

MRS. STEIG: [*Gruff whisper*] Tell the man, Ermintrude! [*Rising*] Go on!

ERMINTRUDE: [*Resolutely*] Don't want to sing!

DOOLEY: [*Beguilingly*] Now, now, Ermintrude, certainly we'll sing! That's what we're here for! [ERMINTRUDE *shakes head and starts to flee.* MRS. STEIG *blocks her way and pushes her C.*]

MRS. STEIG: I can't understand it. Ermintrude sings all the time at home.

DOOLEY: Really?

MRS. STEIG: [*Threateningly*] Maybe if her *father* were here. . . .

DOOLEY: Well, I'm afraid the show must go on. Peg, will you show these ladies off, please? [*Ushers them L.*] Perhaps next week Ermintrude will honor us with. . . .

ERMINTRUDE: [*Suddenly scurries to microphone. Gasping*] "The Man on the Flying Trapeze"!

DOOLEY: [*Pleased*] Well, well! Wonderful!

MRS. STEIG: There we are. Ermintrude knows twelve verses.

Dooley and the Amateur Hour • **1 3 7**

DOOLEY: We'll only have time for five.

ERMINTRUDE: [*Sings five verses. Her voice is adequate. She starts hesitantly—but gains confidence and even asks the audience to join in the last two choruses.*]

DOOLEY: [*Leading applause as he returns C.*] Thanks, Ermintrude. We're mighty glad you've sung for us. *I* couldn't carry a tune if it had handles. And thank you too, Mrs. Steig. [PEGGY *helps* ERMINTRUDE *and* MRS. STEIG *off.*] Now that you've had proof that our amateurs mean business, we'll go on to the next number. [*Consulting list*] It says here that _____ will do a _____. [*Fill in with name and act from your group. If desired, additional numbers may be inserted here.*]

DOOLEY: [*Leading applause as* PERFORMER *leaves stage*] Let's show our appreciation. That was fine! Thank you indeed. And now we have a rare treat for you! A violin solo by Miss Gladys Wiczynski, the talented sister of our famous fullback —your candidate for All-American and mine—Herman Wiczynski! Wahohh! [*Leads enthusiasm.*] Is Herman in the audience?

HERMAN: [*From auditorium*] You bet!

DOOLEY: Step up with Gladdy, Herman, and let the folks see you. [*Applause from audience*] That's right, folks. When you think of Gladys think of Herman. That's what I always do. [HERMAN *escorts* GLADYS, *carrying a violin, to the stage.* PEGGY *assists them.*] Hello there, Herman. I knew you wouldn't miss this. So this is Gladys!

PEGGY: Make Herman do something, Dooley.

DOOLEY: Swell idea. Herman, say a few words to your loyal supporters out there.

HERMAN: [*Into microphone*] Hi!

DOOLEY: Is that all you have to say, Herman? I've heard you say a good deal more than that.

HERMAN: [*Boastfully*] I'm not much on public appearances . . . except on the football field. Little Gladdy here will carry on for the Wiczynskis. Hit 'em where they live, Gladdy! Give 'em _____. [*Fill in with title.* HERMAN *flourishes fist and moves L., shadowboxing.*]

GLADYS: [*Performs violin solo. She is not an inspired player.*]

DOOLEY: [*Leading applause after number*] I always like honest effort. She was *trying,* all right. And don't forget her brother, folks. Her brother's a mighty man! [HERMAN *and* GLADYS *leave stage.*] Let's race right along, ladies and gentlemen. Next performer is _____ in _____. [*Fill in with name and act from your group.*]

DOOLEY: [*Applauding as* PERFORMER *leaves stage*] That's the way to please them! And now, ladies and gentlemen, last—but not least—we have an unusual novelty knockout! Rootin' Tootin' Rollickin' Raymond Parker, a native son and a Troubadour of Tomorrow! Rumor has it Raymond will wow ya! Mosey along up har, Ray. [RAYMOND *comes to stage from audience.*] By the way, folks, Raymond has a pretty keen sister. Stand up and wave, Kitty, so everyone will know you. [KITTY *stands in auditorium. Applause*] Crooners and groaners better look to their laurels 'cause here's Raymond Parker. He's going to sing "Oh, Bury Me Not on the Lone Prairie." What key, Ray—skeleton key? Don't shoot, Ray! I was only fooling! Okay, Ray. Rope 'em and tie 'em and brand 'em the way you want 'em!

RAYMOND: [*Sings. His cause seems hopeless. His voice is bad. His earnest delivery and gestures are comic. The audience laughs.*]

Oh, bury me naht on the lo-one prairie-ee,
Where the wild coyotes will how-w-wl o'er me,
Where the buzzard waits and the wind blows free-ee-ee,
Oh, bury me not on the lo-one prairie-ee!

[*Nervously mops brow, knocking off sombrero.* DOOLEY *retrieves it, dusts it off and replaces it. He smiles encouragement.*]

O lee-oo lay-lay-ee
O lee-oo-lee. Lee.

[RAYMOND'S *yodeling, too, is poor. He struggles on heroically through the next stanza.*]

Where the dew-drop glo-ows and the butterflies re-est,
And the flowers bloom o'er the prairie's crest,
Where the wild coyote and the winds sport free-ee-ee,
Oh, bury me not on the lo-one prairie-ee.

O lee-oo lay-lay-ee.
O lee-oo-lee. Lee.

DOOLEY: [*Good-naturedly*] The only way you can stop a cowboy, folks, is to chop off his head and hide it from him.

RAYMOND: [*Shoving him aside*] Look out! [*Sings.*]

Oh, bury me naht! and his voi-oice failed the-ere,
But they took no heed to his dying prayer,
In a little bahx, just six by three-ee-ee,
His bones now rot on the lo-one prairie-ee.

O lee-oo lay-lay-ee.
O lee-oo-lee. Lee.

Yippeee! [*Bows and struts off while* DOOLEY *leads hearty applause.*]

DOOLEY: That, ladies and gentlemen, winds up the Taj Mahal's amateur program for today. And now will the two judges please step forward? [TWO JUDGES *rise and mount stage.*] We're going to have a mighty hard time deciding, aren't we, folks? See you soon. [DOOLEY *and* TWO JUDGES *exeunt R.*]

PEGGY: [*Into microphone*] While the judges are conferring, we have a professional act for you. It wasn't eligible for the contest, but we're sure you'll enjoy it. May we present _____. [PEGGY *exits L. Fill in with number from your group. If desired, additional numbers—"professional"—may be inserted here.*]

DOOLEY: [*Reentering R. as* PERFORMER *leaves to applause. Purposely rapid*) Only have a moment, folks. Picture's about to begin. Majority vote of the judges gives first prize to Rollickin' Ray Parker! They think he's an up-and-coming comedian! His clowning was superb! Your check's in the manager's office, Raymond. And the passes are there for the other performers. Don't forget, folks, another Amateur Hour next week! Hope you liked it! *On* with the show! [*Blackout as* DOOLEY *hurries L. with microphone*]

PART III

The curtain rises on the lobby of the theater, right after Amateur Hour. PEGGY *and* MRS. BURNSIDE *are beaming and shaking hands.*

MRS. BURNSIDE: Very successful, all around.

DOOLEY: [*Still supercharged, hastening in U.C.*] Well, that's over!

PEGGY: [*Happily*] You were terrific, Jack!

MRS. BURNSIDE: Dooley, I owe you an apology. You did a good

Dooley and the Amateur Hour • **141**

job. I didn't think you had it in you. [*Laughing*] The way you handled that Parker squirt. . . .

DOOLEY: Hm? Oh, yes. I guess I did all right.

MRS. BURNSIDE: You were *fine*. I'm thinking of making you our permanent emcee.

DOOLEY: You're kidding?

MRS. BURNSIDE: Not at all.

DOOLEY: Would a raise go with it?

MRS. BURNSIDE: Yes, Dooley. And a joke book. [*Exits to office.*]

DOOLEY: Well, this is my day! Of course I gave Ray Parker last place myself—but Kitty doesn't know it.

PEGGY: I'd like to be around when she says thanks.

DOOLEY: [*Radiantly*] Oh, I'm looking forward to that li'l ol' moment myself. Pretty lucky, eh? Imagine me an actor, Peg. Want my autograph? Kitty always said a talent scout might show up and spot me while I'm—[KITTY *storms in U.C., dragging* RAYMOND *by the hand.*]

KITTY: [*Shrilly*] Go in the office! Get your check!

RAYMOND: [*Balking*] But Kitty. . . .

KITTY: [*Screaming*] You heard me! Hurry up!

RAYMOND: But I wanted to see the cartoon.

KITTY: Do as I say, you—you lop-eared cowboy! [RAYMOND *shuffles into the office.*] Jack Dooley! I could just simply murder you!

DOOLEY: [*Bleating*] Huhh? What did I do?

KITTY: Don't you even know?

DOOLEY: Raymond won, didn't he?

KITTY: You've made him the laughingstock of town! They laughed at him—giggled their silly heads off—at a *Parker!* At a *Grove Street Parker!*

DOOLEY: Shh! The picture's on. [*Consolingly*] Now, Kitty, that was the only way to. . . .

KITTY: [*Unconsoled*] You're responsible! You and that Troubadour of Tomorrow stuff! You're my Beau of Yesterday! I never want to see you again! Never! Never! Never! [*Slaps DOOLEY's face. RAYMOND emerges from office, waving check.*]

RAYMOND: Look, Kitty, it's fifteen dollars, all right. Wow! Fifteen. . . .

KITTY: [*Savagely*] Come on! [*Yanks him out to street.*]

PEGGY: Well—some gratitude!

DOOLEY: [*Rubbing cheek*] I certainly can pick them.

PEGGY: That's Kitty Parker. I could have told you.

DOOLEY: Wish you had.

PEGGY: [*Breathlessly*] Do you mean that?

DOOLEY: Sure! Say, how about you and me grabbing a soda after the show. [*Hand to cheek*] Ooh!

PEGGY: Does it hurt, Dooley?

DOOLEY: Ooh—Herman. Where's he hiding?

PEGGY: Don't worry about Herman. If you stood up to him he'd back-pedal so fast you couldn't see him for dust.

DOOLEY: He would? [*Considers it.*] No. Not Herman.

PEGGY: Oh, Jack, I thought you were a man.

DOOLEY: I am. But only one. He's like a crowd of people. A dense crowd.

HERMAN: [*Appearing in doorway U.C.*] Hah!

DOOLEY: [*Weakly*] Hah yourself.

HERMAN: [*Nastily*] I'm going to take your spinal column apart and play marbles with it.

DOOLEY: [*Retreating*] Oh, yeah?

HERMAN: Yeah. And what's more . . . I'm going to do it right now!

DOOLEY: Just a minute. There's a lady present. Peggy, wait inside, please.

PEGGY: [*Dolefully*] Oh, Jack!

DOOLEY: [*Showing her out U.C., trying to be chipper*] Don't forget the sodas—if I can still drink one. [*Waves, returns.*]

HERMAN: [*Jerking thumb toward the emergency exit*] And now you step *outside.*

DOOLEY: Can't we talk this thing over? After all, we're classmates and. . . .

HERMAN: [*Bellowing*] I've had enough of your lip today!

DOOLEY: But—but I mustn't leave the lobby. . . .

HERMAN: [*Menacingly*] Outside—you!

DOOLEY: After you.

HERMAN: And come out fightin'! [*Stomps out L.* DOOLEY *starts to follow. There is a tremendous crashing clatter.*]

144 • *Teen Theater*

DOOLEY: [*Astonished*] Gee whiz! Well, what do you know! The burglar trap! [*Exits L. and drags back* HERMAN.]

PEGGY: [*Racing in U.C.*] What happened? Jack! Did you do that?

DOOLEY: More or less. More or less. [*Stoops, fans* HERMAN, *tries to revive him.*]

HERMAN: [*Sitting up, groaning*] Owww! What a wallop! My head's splittin'.

DOOLEY: [*In control now*] There's plenty more where that came from. Did you want to see me about something, Wiczynski?

HERMAN: [*Stumbling to feet*] I—I guess not.

DOOLEY: Funny. I thought you had something to settle with me.

HERMAN: No, no! Just—ah—wanted to say that you did a swell job on the show today.

DOOLEY: Thanks.

HERMAN: Yes, siree. A good fair-and-square decision.

DOOLEY: [*Airily*] Okay, Wiczynski. See you around.

HERMAN: [*Uncomfortably*] Sure—sure thing. I'll go back to Gladdy. [*Exiting U.C.*] I hope I didn't miss the coming attractions!

PEGGY: I knew you could take care of him.

DOOLEY: Once I got around to it I did all right.

PEGGY: [*Happily*] You know, Dooley, you're really an all-around guy!

DOOLEY: You're—you're overwhelming yourself—even if I've been slow noticing it. Say, are you going to the Senior Prom?

PEGGY: I—I think I have a date.

DOOLEY: [*Masterfully*] Forget it. I'm taking you. [*Starts to embrace her, stops.*] Oops, hold it! Any stage-struck brothers or sisters in your family?

PEGGY: No.

DOOLEY: Any trained mice, or dancing dogs, or that kind of thing?

PEGGY: Absolutely not.

DOOLEY: You're my girl! [*Slips arm around her waist.*]

MRS. BURNSIDE: [*Appearing at office door*] Ah-hum. I beg your pardon. [DOOLEY *and* PEGGY *jump apart.*] I was just—uh— just checking to see if the lobby's still here. I heard a crash.

DOOLEY: It was nothing, Mrs. Burnside. Nothing at all. Purely routine.

MRS. BURNSIDE: That's a relief. [*Disappears into office.*]

DOOLEY: Now where were we?

PEGGY: Right here, Dooley! [*They embrace.*]

The Curtain Falls.

NOTES ON STAGING

DOOLEY and the Amateur Hour is like an accordion. You can stretch it, compress it. Depends on the amount of talent you want to parade in the "amateur show" within it. At the same time the comedy is fairly easy to produce.

Another asset: *Dooley's* audiences feel they are part of the play. They rub elbows with actors who sit in the house, get addressed by the emcee, join in the singing and applause. Result? An extra-special aura of friendliness and fellowship.

By the bye, actors performing only in the amateur hour can rehearse individually—very little if their specialties have been pretested. This feature is greatly appreciated when battling assorted demands on time.

In lining up numbers for the amateur hour—and in spacing them—the director should keep an eye cocked for variety. Anyone introduced as "professional" should, of course, be first-rate.

Many kinds of entertainers may be recruited for the amateur show. Possibilities:

1) Singers—popular, classical, ballad—from solo to glee club. Note that the story of the play has RAYMOND PARKER warble "Oh, Bury Me Not on the Lone Prairie," ERMINTRUDE STEIG, "The Man on the Flying Trapeze." These folk ballads appear in many collections. RAYMOND should stick to the wording given in the script. Other singers might well veer toward other types of songs.

2) Dancers—tap, ballet, modern, soft-shoe, folk. Group numbers and/or solos.

3) Monologuists and impersonators.

4) Magicians, acrobats, baton twirlers, etc.

5) Instrumentalists—piano, violin, guitar, accordion, harmonica, what have you. The plot has GLADYS WICZYNSKI play an instrument, not necessarily a violin. Aim for diversity.

Reminder: save seats in the auditorium (scattered) for the cast.

In general, bring enthusiasm and good spirit to *Dooley* and put on a good show!

Acting

JACK DOOLEY is a rewarding role for an actor who delights in the limelight. He is genial, thinks quickly on his feet, and can improvise—within bounds. He is the thread that pulls the play together and, to stretch a figure, ties it up too. As master of ceremonies, he puts others at ease and helps them do their best.

PEGGY is pert, perky, stable. KITTY is rather off base with affected glamour that is not entirely without allure for DOOLEY, the dodo!

RAYMOND, KITTY'S younger brother, can be any age between eight and sixteen. He wins the amateur contest by being funny-ridiculous in an ingratiating sort of way. Since your judges elect the winner, the cards are stacked for him. Still, RAYMOND should amuse. He ought to develop a pseudo-serious delivery of his ballad.

MRS. BURNSIDE can be anywhere between twenty-five and sixty. She is a vigorous, efficient boss.

GLADYS and ERMINTRUDE can be any convenient ages.

The TWO JUDGES have no lines, but humor can be wrung from who they are, how they cross the stage, what they wear. Attention to such details gives polish.

While performers sit with the audience they have a specific job. They lead the laughter and applause. They should clap especially hard for RAYMOND.

Though specialty acts can be rehearsed separately, everybody in the cast should be sure of his cues. And understand clearly his contribution to the play as a whole. In any event, it is a good idea to schedule at least two ensemble rehearsals.

Scenery and Furnishings

Dooley and the Amateur Hour has three parts but requires just one set. It is the outer lobby of a movie theater, which you can prepare simply. Borrow billboards announcing coming attractions from a theater. Use flats, drapes and/or screens (see Guide) to construct the confines of the lobby.

There are three practical doors—to the theater, manager's office, and emergency exit. The fourth exit, leading to the cashier's booth and the street, can be a door, archway, or any opening convenient to your stage. Use backing at any exit the audience can see through, especially upstage where a dark drape will do nicely. Signs can either be attached or painted on doors. The poster reading "TAJ MAHAL THEATER INTRODUCING AMATEUR HOUR TODAY! PRIZES!!!" should have large lettering. It helps spectators grasp the exposition (information needed for understanding the plot). If no ticket box is available, make one by painting or covering a crate.

Notice that the change of scene from the lobby to the theater stage requires merely drawing the front curtain. Play Part II on the apron. For Part III, open the curtain again and you are back in the lobby. So there is little work for stage crews once the set is in place.

Properties

Most theaters have a microphone. If yours does not, borrow one (from a radio or electrical appliance store, school, etc.) and repay with program credit. *Caution:* test your mike before every performance!

Costumes and Make-up

Borrow or improvise DOOLEY'S doorman uniform. PEGGY dresses more simply than the affected KITTY. MRS. BURNSIDE can wear a tailored suit. The adhesive tape on her forehead should be a good size.

Make RAYMOND'S cowboy get-up a walking ad for Western gear. Include a lariat, chaps, spurs, cuffs, sombrero, boots, scarf, holsters, and a loud shirt. Corral them from obliging youngsters or merchants.

GLADYS and ERMINTRUDE can be dressed to look like misfits or straight. MRS. STEIG'S outfit should show unstylish touches like a garish hat and clumpy shoes. Restraint, of course, is advisable.

HERMAN sports a football-letter sweater. Unless the actor is a local gridiron light, pad his shoulders to emphasize bulk.

Encourage amateur-show "contestants" to appear in costumes.

Dooley and the Amateur Hour • 149

They add zing. Dialogue says there has been advance notice, so it is logical for some to be decked out. Make-up also helps many acts.

Special Effects and Lighting

Drop a "crash bag" off stage for the burglar trap that knocks HERMAN out. Use a sturdy canvas or muslin sack and tie in tin, rocks, glass, other noise producers. Experiment. Maybe in your theater a drum, wash basin, or "thunder sheet" will help the clatter.

The sound man of one group thought up a fillip. Whenever the door to the movie theater opened in Part III he played a talking record, simulating a sound track running inside. This detail is certainly no must, but shows what can be done!

Equipment permitting, heighten the dramatic value of specialty numbers by varying the color and kind of lighting. Try following a dancer with a moving spot. Use imagination. Test effects at rehearsals.

Publicity

The large cast should mean lots of word-of-mouth publicity. Remind the cast to talk-it-up. But supplement with a good campaign. If any outstanding talent is to appear, be sure to publicize the fact.

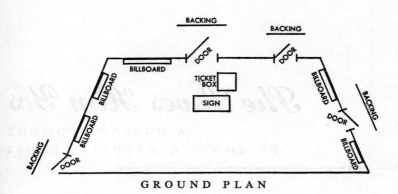

GROUND PLAN

FURNISHINGS	PROPERTIES
billboards	small money bag
sign "TAJ MAHAL THEATER	microphone
INTRODUCING AMATEUR	theater pass
HOUR TODAY! PRIZES!!!"	list of contestants
ticket box	check
sign "MANAGER'S OFFICE"	
(if not painted on door)	
sign "EMERGENCY EXIT"	
(if not painted on door)	
two chairs (carried on by	
DOOLEY and PEGGY)	

She Loves Him Yes

A ONE-ACT COMEDY
BY EDWIN & NATHALIE GROSS

Cast of Characters

JENNIFER BLAKE	a successful author, about twenty-eight. In the play within the play she becomes twenty-three, attractive, vibrant, and brittle.
TOBY SLOAN	friendly, brash, a high-school senior.
APRIL	the Blake maid, matronly, outspoken, part of the family.
MRS. BLAKE	gracious, hospitable, a trifle fluttery. In her forties.
TIM BLAKE	handsome, athletic, a history teacher. About twenty-two.
VICKI BLAKE	pretty, a would-be actress. About twenty.
BUFF BLAKE	a lively, precocious twelve-year-old. Youngest Blake boy.
ELIOT BLAKE	personable but a bit self-important, sports a wispy goatee. About eighteen.
SHIRLEY HAWTHORNE	gushy, romantic, and not very bright. About seventeen.
MR. BLAKE	a newspaper editor. In his forties.

SCENE: Corner of a high-school lounge.

The play within the play occurs a few years ago in the Blake living room on a Sunday afternoon in early fall.

As the play begins, the stage apron lights up down right but the curtain does not rise. JENNIFER BLAKE *enters from off right in a tailored suit and hat, carrying a portfolio. She looks around this corner of a school lounge. She sits on the only piece of furniture, a bench stage right.* TOBY SLOAN *bustles down the left side aisle of the theater to the apron and across the stage.*

JENNIFER: [*Rising*] Looking for me?

TOBY: Hope I didn't keep you waiting. Just had gym. Say, you are Miss Blake, aren't you—Jennifer Blake, the author?

JENNIFER: [*Pleasantly*] Yes, I am.

TOBY: Excuse my stare. [*Shaking hands*] I'm Toby Sloan. Never met the writer of a best seller before!

JENNIFER: [*Smiling*] My paragraphs don't show, do they, Toby?

TOBY: It's really swell of you to come speak to us. I'm editor of the school magazine, so I'm elected to escort you to Assembly.

JENNIFER: It's nice to meet you.

TOBY: Thanks. Want to sit down, Miss Blake? [JENNIFER *sits on bench. Foot on bench, resting elbow on knee*] You know, you're our most famous graduate.

JENNIFER: [*Protestingly*] Oh, Toby, there are so many others. . . .

TOBY: Well—for me you're tops. I'm planning to follow in your footsteps.

She Loves Him Yes • **153**

JENNIFER: That's good to hear, Toby.

TOBY: [*Self-consciously*] If I can. [*Sighs and moves about nervously.*]

JENNIFER: Have you done much writing, Toby?

TOBY: Oh yes. [*Steeling himself*] As a matter of fact, I'd like to consult you on a professional matter.

JENNIFER: Have we time?

TOBY: Uh-huh. They told you to come early to make sure you wouldn't be late. Here's the point, Miss Blake. I recently finished my first long story. And do you know what my English teacher says? It depends too much on coincidence! Isn't she way off? Don't the strangest things happen just by chance?

JENNIFER: Sometimes.

TOBY: Certainly! I said, "Miss Benson, look at Oliver Cromwell. He won the Battle of Dunbar on a September third, the Battle of Worcester on a September third, and he died on a September third."

JENNIFER: And what did Miss Benson say?

TOBY: She said, "It can happen in history, but it *can't* happen here."

JENNIFER: She was undoubtedly right, Toby. Everyone likes to shake hands with the long arm of coincidence. But it's risky business. Here, I'll tell you a story about my own family. It's true as true but I don't plan to use it. [*Patting bench*] I think you'll see why. [TOBY *sits.*] Well, Toby, a few years ago we Blakes lived in a rambling old house here in town. There were five children—and such individualists! You see, Dad was a newspaper editor and quite a cut-up. His motto was "Express yourself!" Even April, our maid, caught the fever.

Why, she became the best Ping-pong player in the neighborhood. [*The curtain rises revealing the* BLAKE *living room on an afternoon a few years ago. It is the pleasantly furnished meeting ground of a sprightly, imaginative family. An entrance up right leads to a hall. A door at stage left leads to the kitchen. A window is open at right. Prominent are a sofa and coffee table R.C., a table U.L.C., a chair and hassock L.C., a chair D.L. There is a mirror on the wall at L. Chairs, lamps, end tables, and bookcases round out the décor. At the moment* APRIL *is removing runners from the table U.L. C. She spreads a tablecloth.*] On this particular Sunday afternoon Dad was at the newspaper office. As for Mom—well, her job was tying us all up into one family. [*Lights on* JENNIFER *and* TOBY *fade.* APRIL *exits L.* MRS. BLAKE *enters U.R. She comes from the street and carries flowers. She sits and arranges them in bowl on coffee table.*]

MRS. BLAKE: [*Calling*] April. Eliot here yet?

APRIL: [*Entering L. with tray with dishes and glasses*] No sign of him, Mrs. Blake. [*Starts setting table U.L.C. for buffet snack.*]

MRS. BLAKE: [*Indicating flowers*] How do you like these?

APRIL: Rather nice.

MRS. BLAKE: Buff's through washing the car. Now he's oiling his bike. Don't let him track up the house.

APRIL: [*Emphatically*] I won't, Mrs. Blake. What girl is Eliot bringing this afternoon?

MRS. BLAKE: [*Worriedly*] I don't know. She's from out of town. He kept saying he'd be late for the concert if he stopped by with her.

APRIL: Hm! I'm glad Mr. Blake *insists* the children introduce their friends. No telling who Eliot will date!

MRS. BLAKE: You're right, April.

APRIL: He's changing since he likes classical music. That goatee he's nourishing——

MRS. BLAKE: [*Laughing*] Back to Brahms or something——

APRIL: Well, maybe someday he'll find a girl like that Anne Saunders Tim used to go with.

MRS. BLAKE: [*Wistfully*] Perhaps—someday.

APRIL: Now there was a sweet young thing. Tim should have married her—no matter what.

MRS. BLAKE: I'm afraid it was out of our hands, April. [*Crosses U.L.C. and places flower bowl on table as centerpiece.*] There we are. Please call me when Eliot comes.

APRIL: Okay, Mrs. Blake. [MRS. BLAKE *exits U.R. Soon as* APRIL *is alone she rearranges flowers, exits L. Lights come up on* JENNIFER *and* TOBY.]

JENNIFER: Well, Toby, I was the oldest child and next was my brother Tim. He was a new history teacher—right in this high school—and a disappointed lover. You see, he'd been planning all through college to marry Anne Saunders. But they had an argument right before graduation—and Anne went home to Los Angeles. Next we heard Anne was engaged to somebody else. [APRIL *enters L., and sets platter of doughnuts on table.*] Tim was terribly upset about it. But he tried not to show it. [*Lights on* JENNIFER *and* TOBY *fade.* TIM *swoops in U.R., wearing bathrobe over casual clothes.*]

TIM: [*Grabbing* APRIL *around the waist*] My dream girl! How can I study ancient history when you are near?

APRIL: Let me go, Tim Blake—or you'll wish you were ancient!

TIM: [*Releasing her*] What's good to eat, April? I'm starr-ving!

APRIL: That's what young teachers are supposed to do. Now no sampling. Your brother's bringing a new ladyfriend in.

TIM: Not another? [*Grabs doughnut.* APRIL *swats his wrist, retrieves doughnut.*]

APRIL: Use up all your energy eating! How'll you think up a good history test?

TIM: [*Reaching again*] *You* are the true creative spirit in the Blake house.

APRIL: [*Intercepting*] Hogwash doesn't work with me.

TIM: [*Mock menacingly*] When I waste away and die my ghost'll haunt you!

APRIL: Not if my broom's handy. Now go back to your room and work!

TIM: You're a tyrant—but I love you! Farewell, my own true heart! [*Snares doughnut and runs out U.R.* APRIL *stomps out L.* VICKI *wanders in U.R. in sport clothes. She is about twenty and pretty. She carries a book and gestures, speaking soundlessly. She crosses to mirror and continues pantomime, watching herself and occasionally referring to book.* APRIL *enters L. with fruit and popcorn. She blandly disregards* VICKI *and deposits them on table. Lights come up on* JENNIFER *and* TOBY.]

JENNIFER: My sister Vicki was President of the Drama League at the "U." She used to drift around the house memorizing her parts. [*Lights on* JENNIFER *and* TOBY *fade.* VICKI *leans closer to mirror.*]

She Loves Him Yes • **157**

VICKI: Good thing people don't see an actress this close. Oh, but I guess they do in the movies. And in television.

APRIL: What's the play this week?

VICKI: *The Frozen Clock.*

APRIL: Well, I declare!

VICKI: I'm supposed to limp in it. I'm the heroine. April, do you know how to limp?

APRIL: You an actress and you don't know that?

VICKI: I'm not sure of myself. Wish I'd seen the play on Broadway. [*Limping uncertainly*] How would you do it?

APRIL: Well, honey, there was my Uncle Steven. He had himself a fancy step. Like this. [*Demonstrates.*]

VICKI: Oh, no. This girl's very delicate.

APRIL: My delicate days are over, honey.

VICKI: I mean I mustn't overact. Look, I'm nineteen and poor. I live in Chicago.

APRIL: That's got nothing to do with limping.

VICKI: Just background, April. Make believe I have a huge audience out there. [*Seizes* APRIL'S *hand, leads her to footlights, points.*] In a lovely theater.

APRIL: [*Dogmatically*] I'm not so hot at pretending, but I'll cooperate. [*Staring front*] That usher better stop talking. And that gentleman over there! It's too dark to read the program, mister.

VICKI: [*Carried away*] The audience sees me and feels sympathy for all the lonely people in the world!

APRIL: How much are the tickets?

VICKI: [*Mood broken*] Oh—April!

APRIL: [*Limping*] Say, how about something like this?

VICKI: Not bad. [*Limping out U.R.*] Well, I'll work on it. Thanks.

APRIL: [*Grinning*] Ha! There's life in the old girl yet! [*Limps out L. Lights come up on* JENNIFER *and* TOBY.]

JENNIFER: I ought to tell you about myself, Toby. I was out of college and trying to write. I worked like fury in those days. Every now and then I invaded the living room for relaxation. [*Rising*] Or inspiration. [JENNIFER *quickly removes her hat and jacket, and takes a writing board and pencil from her portfolio. In sweater and skirt, she enters the living-room frame. The lights on* TOBY *black out. He disappears.* JENNIFER *stands at C., writing.* APRIL *enters L. with cookies and nuts.*] April, would you say "sesquicentennial."

APRIL: Sesquicentennial. [JENNIFER *frowns, shakes head.*] What you after, Jen?

JENNIFER: I want someone in my story to mispronounce it.

APRIL: How about "sesasquicentennial"? Stick an extra syllable in. [JENNIFER *writes. Peering over her shoulder*] And underline it.

JENNIFER: That does it. [*Sits and concentrates on work. Telephone rings off L.*]

APRIL: [*Exiting L.*] It sure is lucky for this family I know about everything! [BUFF *enters U.R. He is about twelve and wears a sweatshirt over a bathing suit.* APRIL *is heard calling off L.*] Mrs. Blake! Telephone!

BUFF: Can I talk, Sis, or are you working?

JENNIFER: Talk away.

APRIL: [*Looking in L.*] Buff, are you greasy?

BUFF: No, Your Highness. [APRIL *disappears. Annoyed, glaring toward window*] Boy, what a fathead!

JENNIFER: [*Amused*] What's eating you?

BUFF: I just stood inspection. Eliot and his date. Jeepers!

JENNIFER: [*Rising*] Where are they now?

BUFF: Admiring the view. Wait'll you see her. A kewpie doll. He simpers, "This is our fledgling." And she giggles, "Oh, how cute!"

JENNIFER: Really?

BUFF: I felt like saying "da-da." Eliot has plenty to learn about females! [*Helps himself to nuts and cookies.*]

JENNIFER: [*Amused*] You're right, fledgling. But listen. Who set my alarm for four-thirty this morning?

BUFF: [*Innocently*] Don't ask me.

JENNIFER: [*Sternly*] No play-acting. C'mon. Were you in on it?

BUFF: Why, I'd never do that to you, Jen.

JENNIFER: Well, I guess you didn't think of it. Tell me—did Eliot go out last night?

BUFF: No. He was the only one home. [*Quickly*] But I'm not a snitcher.

JENNIFER: Thank you, Buff. Eliot's never learned to be subtle, has he? Now how'll I get even?

BUFF: [*Loftily*] Say. Did anyone ever tell you revenge is stupid?

JENNIFER: [*Sharply*] What?

BUFF: Psychologists agree on it. It's immature.

JENNIFER: [*Mock angry*] Go away, professor!

BUFF: [*Avidly*] On the other hand, Eliot Casanova Blake should fall down a couple of pegs.

JENNIFER: Now we're cooking! [*Rubbing hands with glee*] Ahh! His taste in women shall be his undoing! A kewpie doll, you say? Let's go to work on her.

BUFF: [*Ruefully*] Can't. I'm on my good behavior.

JENNIFER: What's it this time? Don't tell me! I'll see you later. [*Exits U.R.* BUFF *practices an elaborate pitching windup.*]

MRS. BLAKE: [*Off*] Buff! [*Coming on L.*] Buff Blake!

BUFF: Yes, Mom?

MRS. BLAKE: Judge Anderson just phoned me.

BUFF: He did?

MRS. BLAKE: He says your team broke two of his windows this morning. Two!

BUFF: Oh, you know the Judge is an old fuddy-dud! [APRIL *enters L., sets silverware and napkins on table. She lingers, eaves-dropping.*]

MRS. BLAKE: That's not the point. How did it happen?

BUFF: Was simple. We were playing ball near the Judge's house. I hit one and it cracked a window. We'd never broken any over there before—so we went right on. And—uh . . . next time I got up I smacked another. See?

MRS. BLAKE: [*Wearily*] Yes.

BUFF: The law of averages went back on us. Guess it doesn't work Sundays. [*Forces a laugh.*]

MRS. BLAKE: There's nothing funny. [APRIL *covers a chuckle and escapes L.*] I don't know what Dad'll say. You're lucky he's a baseball fan.

BUFF: Team's collecting money this afternoon. We'll meet our legal obligations.

MRS. BLAKE: [*Sighing*] The Judge made it a moral issue. He lectured on decorum. . . .

BUFF: Didn't I tell you I'm going to be a veterinarian? Decorum's not my strong point.

MRS. BLAKE: Buff Blake, promise me—[*Throwing up hands*] Well, just try to behave! [*Gazing out window*] Is *that* the girl Eliot's dating? Goodness. She looks—er . . . fluffy.

BUFF: Slushy's the word, Mom.

MRS. BLAKE: Buff! Go get dressed. You can't meet Eliot's friend like that.

BUFF: I've already met her. Can't I be excused?

MRS. BLAKE: I'll expect you in ten minutes.

BUFF: [*Exiting U.R. carrying robe*] Ah me, some day I'll have a bachelor apartment!

MRS. BLAKE: [*Calling*] April, is everything ready?

APRIL: [*Looking in L.*] Ready *and* waiting. [*Disappears L.*]

MRS. BLAKE: I'll get Eliot. [*Calling through window*] Eliot—Eliot, dear.

ELIOT: [*Off, too sweetly*] Be right with you, Mother. [ELIOT BLAKE *and* SHIRLEY HAWTHORNE *enter U.R.* ELIOT *is eighteen and somewhat ill-at-ease. He wears a suit and sports a wispy goatee.* SHIRLEY, *seventeen and gushy, is fussily dressed.*]

Hello, Mother. Mother, may I present Shirley Hawthorne, a visitor from California. Shirley, my mother.

SHIRLEY: How do you do, Mrs. Blake. I've been just dying to meet you. Eliot's told me all about you.

MRS. BLAKE: How do you do, Shirley. I'm so glad you could come. Won't you sit down?

ELIOT: Good idea, Mom. [*Escorts* SHIRLEY *to sofa. They sit.*] We don't have much time. You shouldn't have bothered with things.

MRS. BLAKE: [*Graciously*] Oh, it's no bother, Eliot. [*Sitting*] It's a bit cloudy today. Did the view from the hill impress you?

SHIRLEY: Oh, it was wonderful. It took my breath away. I told Eliot I'm just the luckiest girl to be visiting this gorgeous town.

MRS. BLAKE: What part of California are you from, Shirley?

SHIRLEY: Los Angeles. But I'm not one of those who only talks about California. I like other places, too. Don't you think we should all be broadminded?

MRS. BLAKE: Er—uh—yes, I do.

ELIOT: Mom, Shirley's been in forty-eight out of the forty-three states—no, no—I mean forty-three of the forty-eight. [*Titters.*] Isn't that the way it went, Shirley? [APRIL *enters L. carrying platter of tea sandwiches. Sets them on table U. L.C.*]

SHIRLEY: [*Cooing*] Yes, Eliot. You've a wonderful memory.

ELIOT: Oh, Shirley, this is April.

SHIRLEY: How do you do. Eliot's told me all about you.

APRIL: Howdy. [*Shrugs, exits L.*]

ELIOT: Mom, did you know California has the highest and lowest altitudes in the United States?

MRS. BLAKE: I suppose I've never thought about it.

VICKI: [*Limping in U.R. singing*] Here I come limping, limping, limping—Mother darling, I'm learning the most beautiful part! I'm a neglected, lonely cripple. It's terrific—but awfully wearing.

MRS. BLAKE: Doughnuts will pep you up, dear.

VICKI: [*Noticing* SHIRLEY] Oh, company. 'Lo. Like my new limp? [*Demonstrating*] Neat, eh?

ELIOT: [*Smirking*] Kind of lame.

SHIRLEY: It's so convincing. It's absolutely realistic!

VICKI: Huh? [*Sizing up* SHIRLEY] Glad you like it. It isn't perfect yet.

SHIRLEY: Personally, I've always wanted to act. It's my secret ambition.

VICKI: Yes? [*Sits on hassock.*]

SHIRLEY: Why, you must be Vicki. The President of the Drama League! Eliot's told me all about you.

MRS. BLAKE: Yes, Shirley, this is my daughter Vicki. Vicki, Shirley Hawthorne. [VICKI *nods.*]

ELIOT: Shirley's a house guest of Professor Steiner's.

SHIRLEY: It's so wonderful living with a real professor. I'm thrilled to death.

VICKI: Are you enrolled at the University?

SHIRLEY: No. But I'm studying so hard to pass those entrance exams. Some day I'll be there with you! [APRIL *enters L. carrying jug of cider. She serves.*]

ELIOT: I hope you like cider. We always serve it.

SHIRLEY: Why, I just adore it.

MRS. BLAKE: Have you any brothers and sisters?

SHIRLEY: Oh, no, Mrs. Blake. There's only me and Mummy and Daddy. But I have jillions of friends.

MRS. BLAKE: [*Wistfully*] A small family must be restful.

BUFF: [*Entering U.R. in softball uniform lettered "Wildcats"*] Hi, everybody.

MRS. BLAKE: Is that the only suit you could find, Buff?

BUFF: It was handy.

MRS. BLAKE: Shirley, you've met Buff?

SHIRLEY: Yes, and Eliot's told me all about his big little brother.

BUFF: [*Annoyed*] Can I see if the car is dry?

MRS. BLAKE: Never mind, Buff. Give April a hand.

BUFF: [*Resigned*] Okay, chief.

ELIOT: [*Nervously*] We'll have to leave for the concert in a few minutes, Mother.

SHIRLEY: Oh, but we're having such a lovely visit. It was so kind of you to have me over.

VICKI: [*No longer interested*] Pardon me, all.

BUFF: Can I be excused too, Mom?

MRS. BLAKE: I'll tell you when.

JENNIFER: [*Off*] Buff! Buff, are you there? [*Floats in U.R. with preoccupied air wearing what might once have been a curtain draped around her like an old-fashioned gown. She carries her writing board and pencil. Studiously ignoring company*] Oh, Buff, do me a favor. Find me a garden snail. I'm writing about one and I can't remember—— Yummy, doughnuts! Skip it. [*Biting one*] Mmmm! [*Pretending to spy* ELIOT] Elly! I didn't know you were home!

ELIOT: [*Scowling*] Shirley, my sister Jen. The writer.

SHIRLEY: How do you do, Jennifer. Eliot's told me all about you.

JENNIFER: Oh, I hope not.

SHIRLEY: [*Giggling*] Well, he's said a heap of nice things.

JENNIFER: [*Confidingly*] Has he told you about *himself?* It's very creeepy. See, when no one's looking, Eliot and his goatee prowl through the house till they find alarm clocks——

ELIOT: Hush up, Jen!

JENNIFER: Shirley'd love to know about you, I'm sure. And Elly has lots of other peculiarities. Now, for instance——

ELIOT: [*Irritated*] Mom, send her packing, will you? Or make her take that curtain off.

JENNIFER: But Elly, you know the whole family's tetched.

ELIOT: Eat another doughnut, will ya, pul-lease?

MRS. BLAKE: Dad and I have always encouraged self-expression in the children. Maybe if we had it to do again. . . . [*Shakes head.* JENNIFER *sits, covers face with her hands and experiments removing them in peek-a-boo fashion.*]

BUFF: Go on, Mrs. B., you love it.

ELIOT: [*Self-consciously*] You never know what Jen'll wear or do or say next.

BUFF: Depends on the character she's writing. What's it today, Jen?

JENNIFER: A nineteenth-century bride.

SHIRLEY: Oh my goodness—that's exciting!

JENNIFER: Oops! Excuse please. An idea! [*Starts writing. APRIL gawks over JENNIFER'S shoulder. VICKI wanders in L., practicing her limp.*]

ELIOT: Just ignore the sideshow.

SHIRLEY: I think it's absolutely wonderful. It's so thrilling to see you all. My goodness, lucky lucky me. Your snacks are *delicious,* April.

APRIL: Thank you. [*Exits L. Shrill whistle sounds off R.*]

BUFF: [*Shouting off*] Coming! Excuse, everybody. It was a pleasure.

MRS. BLAKE: Where are you going?

BUFF: Legal obligations. [*Runs out U.R. VICKI sits.*]

ELIOT: Don't you think we'd better get going——

JENNIFER: [*Looking up, determined to tease*] Shirley, could you help me with a case history? Could you tell me why you dated Eliot?

SHIRLEY: [*Eagerly*] Why of course I'll help you. Professor Steiner said he was a fine boy.

JENNIFER: Yes?

SHIRLEY: And—uh—he rather appealed to me.

JENNIFER: Do you mean he has animal magnetism?

SHIRLEY: Well, if you want to put it that way. Yes, he does!

ELIOT: [*Upset*] Cut it out, Jen!

JENNIFER: Shirley doesn't mind. Now about the goatee. Did that have anything to do with it? Wait a minute—I need a fresh page.

SHIRLEY: Let me think. I want to be absolutely truthful.

TIM: [*Swooping in U.R. minus bathrobe*] Hi, everyone! [*Exits L.*]

JENNIFER: Poof—he's gone!

ELIOT: [*Wearily*] That was my big brother——

SHIRLEY: I know. Tim. You've told me all about——

VICKI: Too bad Dad isn't home. You'd know us all.

APRIL: [*Off L.*] Put that thing down!

TIM: [*Off L.*] No. [*Crash off. Scrubbing brush flies through doorway L.*]

APRIL: [*Off L.*] I'm sorry I missed you! [*Sponge flies in.*]

TIM: [*Runs in L. laughing triumphantly and carrying large mixing bowl. Looking back, frenziedly*] Don't throw it—— NO!

APRIL: [*Entering L. brandishing skillet*] I'd like to tom-tom your hide! Give me that!

TIM: Here, catch! [*Fakes throw.* APRIL *squeals.* TIM *passes her bowl.* APRIL *stomps out L.*]

MRS. BLAKE: Tim, I do wish you wouldn't tease April so much. [*Telephone rings off.*]

TIM: Tease *her!* I'm the soul of responsibility. I was going to sponge down my rug where I spilled some ink. [*Sits.*]

MRS. BLAKE: Well, ask permission before you take things.

ELIOT: Don't mind the commotion, Shirley.

SHIRLEY: [*Earnestly*] My, doesn't he look familiar. I know I know him from some place.

APRIL: [*Looking in L.*] Vicki, telephone.

VICKI: Thanks. [*Limps out L.*]

ELIOT: This is Shirley Hawthorne, Tim.

TIM: Welcome! What a get-up, Jen!

JENNIFER: Nineteenth-century bride.

TIM: If you're seeking a worthy candidate to pose as the groom, I offer you——

JENNIFER: Not you!

TIM: Heaven forbid! My brother Eliot. Come, boy, on your feet. With that goatee—and a few touches——

ELIOT: Control yourself. I've a guest.

TIM: I'm sure she'll understand. Won't you, Miss . . . ?

SHIRLEY: [*Eagerly*] Hawthorne—Shirley Hawthorne. Of course I'd understand, Tim.

ELIOT: Well, I'm sorry to spoil your fun, [*Rising*] but we have to get a move on. [MRS. BLAKE *rises.*]

SHIRLEY: [*Rising*] I wish I knew where I've seen you before, Tim Blake. You look. . . .

VICKI: [*Storming in L., limp forgotten*] Eliot! Did you lend my make-up kit to the Rally Committee?

ELIOT: Er—yes—they needed grease paint.

VICKI: Well, they've used mine up and need some more. Now you can begin hunting for some for *them—and for me.* [APRIL *enters L. with fresh doughnuts.*]

SHIRLEY: Grease paint! Just the name thrills me! Did you hear about the new kind they've developed for television? [*Light dawning*] Telev—that's it. Tim—Tim Blake. I saw you on TV.

TIM: Oh yes—that street interview during vacation.

SHIRLEY: [*Seriously*] I remember it very clearly! I was at my best friend's house in Hollywood, and she almost died when she saw you on that screen. She said you're the fellow her cousin Anne Saunders is in love with. . . .

TIM: [*Rising*] Hey, what's going on? A put-up joke?

SHIRLEY: It's no joke. Absolutely not!

TIM: [*Gruffly*] Well, why say Anne's in love with me? She's marrying someone else.

SHIRLEY: Oh no—there's no one else now. My friend says Anne won't even go out with anybody. She just looks at your picture and pines away. . . .

TIM: You're not stringing me along?

SHIRLEY: My goodness, I wouldn't kid about—*this!* The minute you came in I knew I'd seen you before and. . . . Oh, it's so romantic!

TIM: [*Seriously*] Now you're sure?

SHIRLEY: [*Solemnly*] Why, certainly.

TIM: [*Lightly, kissing her brow*] I adore you! [*Sits, reflecting.*]

SHIRLEY: Eliot, isn't it just too exciting?

JENNIFER: Quite a coincidence.

MRS. BLAKE: Yes, indeed.

ELIOT: Well, coincidence or not, we have to go! Come on, Shirley.

SHIRLEY: Well, good-by, everybody.

VICKI: Good-by, Shirley.

JENNIFER: Good-by, kids.

SHIRLEY: Mrs. Blake, I can't tell you how happy I am I came this afternoon. I'll never forget that I was the one who saw Tim on television and—[*Exits U.R. with* MRS. BLAKE *and* ELIOT.]

VICKI: I'll bet she never will forget. [APRIL *starts clearing table.*]

TIM: [*Soberly*] Can I believe a nit-wit like that?

JENNIFER: Well, allowing for exaggeration. . . .

TIM: I'd take the next train if I thought Anne wanted me. . . .

VICKI: Telephone and find out!

TIM: I'll do it! Long-distance, here I come! [*Starts to exit L. Returning, nervously*] What should I say to her?

JENNIFER: Write your own lines, brother. [*Slips off curtain.*]

APRIL: [*Grinning*] I'll help, honey.

TIM: *You* stay here! [*Exits L.*]

MRS. BLAKE: [*Entering U.R.*] Well, of all things!

JENNIFER: Beats my concoctions.

VICKI: Ra-mona! What if Shirley's all wrong?

MRS. BLAKE: I never thought of that.

JENNIFER: We'll know soon enough. Tim's phoning Anne now.

She Loves Him Yes • **171**

APRIL: This Blake family isn't easy to forget. She's waiting for him.

SHIRLEY: [*Running in U.R. followed by* ELIOT. *Breathlessly*] I just remembered! Anne's wastebasket often has letters to Tim— that she's torn up. I thought he might like to know. . . .

MRS. BLAKE: I'll tell him, Shirley.

ELIOT: [*Yanking* SHIRLEY'S *hand*] Come on! Let's *go!*

SHIRLEY: [*Sweetly*] Good-by again!

MRS. BLAKE and JENNIFER: Good-by. [ELIOT *and* SHIRLEY *exeunt U.R.*]

VICKI: [*Moving L.*] I'd really like to do some eavesdropping.

APRIL: [*Starting L. with loaded tray*] Well, I got an excuse. . . .

MRS. BLAKE: Now, now. Let's be calm and. . . .

TIM: [*Running in L. Excitedly*] Whatdayaknow? [*Waltzing* VICKI *around*] She loves me! She loves me!

VICKI: What'd she say?

TIM: She was out. I spoke to her mother. Where's my valise? I've got to pack!

MRS. BLAKE: Relax, Tim. We'll help you.

TIM: I'll be packed before you know it. [*Races out U.R.* JENNI-FER *starts working away on her writing board.*]

MRS. BLAKE: [*Sighing*] This is a bit sudden.

VICKI: You're taking it well, Mother.

APRIL: [*Exiting L. with tray*] Don't ever let me say anything about Eliot's ladyfriends.

VICKI: This one had merits.

JENNIFER: [*Looking up momentarily*] Still, if he'd shave he'd attract a more intellectual type.

MRS. BLAKE: [*Benignly*] Well, Shirley's young. And sort of sweet. . . .

TIM: [*Bounding in U.R. in undershirt*] April! April!

APRIL: [*Entering L.*] What is it, Romeo?

TIM: Did you iron my shirts?

APRIL: Yep. If I'd known you were going courting, there'd be pink rosettes on 'em.

TIM: None of your lip, Cupid. [*Steering* APRIL *out L.*] Please get them. Make it snappy! Mom, will you phone the principal I might miss a class? And if I bring back a wife you won't mind—I hope.

MRS. BLAKE: [*Tearfully*] Oh, Tim, I'm so very happy for you. I'm so happy I'm cry-ying!

JENNIFER: [*Looking up*] Tim, what are you thinking of right now —right this minute?

TIM: Anne's a beast and an angel. Try to make sense out of that. [JENNIFER *writes.*]

APRIL: [*Entering L.*] Here you are, Romeo. [*Handing him shirts*] Good luck to you, son! [*Hugs him.*]

TIM: Thanks, April. [*Exits U.R.*]

VICKI: I'll kibitz. [*Follows* TIM *off.* APRIL *clears table.*]

MRS. BLAKE: [*Wiping eyes*] Dear, dear, I never thought when I sat there arranging those flowers. . . .

JENNIFER: Mom, can you put into words how *you* feel?

MRS. BLAKE: [*Reprovingly*] Jen! You're not writing all this down, are you?

JENNIFER: [*Nodding*] Notes for future reference. Drama in the raw or something.

MRS. BLAKE: What a family! [*Spying through window*] Why, there's your father! [*Calling*] Dad, I've news for you! [*To* JENNIFER] I'm so glad he's come!

MR. BLAKE: [*Entering U.R.*] Hi, girls.

JENNIFER: Hi, Popsy. [MR. BLAKE *removes overcoat, revealing a football uniform.*]

MRS. BLAKE: *What* happened to you?

MR. BLAKE: Oh, nothing. I stopped at the field to scrimmage with the boys. The coach lent me some duds. Then someone walked off with mine. These feel comfy, though. Now what's the news?

MRS. BLAKE: Oh, we had a little "nothing" of our own. Right in this room!

MR. BLAKE: Let's have the who, what, when, and why.

MRS. BLAKE: Tim will tell you. Come along, Dad.

MR. BLAKE: At your service, Mother. [*Follows* MRS. BLAKE *out U.R.*]

APRIL: I say it and say it again. Living with the Blakes is like being with a circus. [*Exits L. with tray.* JENNIFER, *writing, rises and strolls D.R. out of the living-room frame.* APRIL *reenters, humming, and removes tablecloth. The curtain falls. Lights come up, finding* JENNIFER *and* TOBY *on bench D.R.* JENNIFER *again wears jacket.*]

JENNIFER: There's the coincidence, Toby. It walked right into our living room and helped marry off my brother.

TOBY: I get your point, Miss Blake. [*School bell rings. Grinning and rising*] And would you call it a coincidence the bell for Assembly just rang?

JENNIFER: [*Smiling*] I certainly would.

TOBY: I'll wait for you after your speech. [*Starting L.*] Say, if my English teacher corners you, put in a kind word for me. Maybe I ought to start writing about *my* family. We're sort of wacky, too! [TOBY and JENNIFER, *carrying hat and portfolio, exeunt L.*]

As the Play Ends.

NOTES ON STAGING

SHE Loves Him Yes highlights the capers of a large, relaxed family. The mood is exuberant good-humored. And there are lusty roles for all.

A gimmick in the staging: there is a "play within a play." JENNIFER tells a story and steps into it as it unfolds on stage. No special equipment is needed for the effect. Even groups with limited facilities can enjoy working it out.

Acting

The BLAKES have a strong sense of family tie. They treat each other with spoofing yet gracious familiarity. APRIL, like many a long-time maid, has an "interferiority" complex. But the BLAKES love her. She may be played as Irish, Swedish, German, etc. But *avoid* caricature!

The BLAKES have undoubtedly seen many years in their house. They should act at home in that living room.

The actress playing JEN has to "stretch." At first she's a successful author. She becomes younger, an unheralded writer in the story she tells TOBY.

JEN'S return to the stage apron near the end should be smooth. While attention is on APRIL, she slips her jacket on in the dark, stows her writing board in her portfolio—and when the lights find her is again the noted author!

TOBY, though supposedly listening to the story, should slip off stage once JEN enters the living room. He should return to the apron unobtrusively just before she rejoins him. This device is often used in plays. The audience rarely notices, accepts it if it does.

TIM is the romantic lead. His charm makes his good luck satisfying to the audience.

For her role in a college play, VICKI is learning to limp. In no way is she mocking an infirmity, so do not exaggerate.

ELIOT is caught up in a stuffy period which, being a BLAKE, he will probably outgrow. He is also at a disadvantage since he is straining to maintain poise while introducing SHIRLEY to the family.

SHIRLEY, gushy and terribly-eager-to-say-the-right-thing, is still attractive and sweet. But she is a comic character, and an actress should develop the fun in the part.

BUFF can be switched to a girl's role if more convenient, or his age changed. But remember that someone older can act him.

At rehearsals the cast should grow used to handling the food, passing, balancing, nibbling. No fancy juggling, though—it is just a teatime snack.

Scenery and Furnishings

Most of the play occurs in the BLAKE living room. Some scenes use the apron to suggest a corner of a high-school lounge, with the only furnishing a bench down right. Required, then, is *one* set. Simple!

For the living-room confines use flats, drapes and/or screens (see Guide). Remember backing if your audience can see through window and doors. The window, any size, need not be practical. If you wish, you can substitute an archway for the door up right. (By the way, *Date-Time's* scenery is similar. Saved those flats?)

The BLAKE décor is attractive, has a lived-in feel. Borrow basic furnishings (from a store, home, second-hand dealer, etc.). Spruce up as needed. Fill in with cheery details. Mold the scene into the meeting ground of a sprightly household.

Bookcases are mentioned for the room but are optional.

The mirror should be coated with soap, or simulated with silver paper or paint on cardboard. No distracting reflections wanted!

Properties

A few platters of snacks are set out, but little need be eaten. Shape imitation food out of cardboard and papier-mâché, and top with edibles.

Perhaps local gardens will yield MRS. BLAKE's flowers. Maybe a florist will, for program credit. Also, artificial ones will do, and these last through all performances.

JEN takes writing board (any clipboard) and pencil from a portfolio. Do not forget paper on the board.

Costumes and Make-up

JEN wears a smart suit and hat. She loses years as she doffs her hat and jacket, revealing a youthful sweater on entering the living room. The curtain she dresses up in can be of any material. It need not look too incongruous.

TOBY has on everyday school clothes.

APRIL is clad in a neat housedress or maid's uniform. She ought to appear matronly so TIM's joshing is not misconstrued.

BUFF wears a sweatshirt over a bathing suit, changes to a soft-ball uniform. Its "WILDCATS" lettering can be changed or omitted.

She Loves Him Yes • **177**

MRS. BLAKE dresses attractively. Consult the Guide about her middle-age make-up, also MR. BLAKE'S. His football togs should be easy to borrow.

TIM and VICKI are dressed casually. ELIOT, in a suit, and SHIRLEY, in a dating frock, are turned out more formally.

About ELIOT'S goatee: if your actor does not grow his own wispy beard, fashion it from artificial crepe hair. The Guide advises on application and removal. At rehearsals ELIOT should get used to its feel, the cast to seeing him with it.

Special Effects and Lighting

A telephone rings twice off stage. (Suggestions are listed under Special Effects in the Guide.)

For the school bell, arrange to ring the real thing if one is in the building. Otherwise use batteries wired to a bell, or a record.

The off-stage noise heard while TIM raids the kitchen is never identified. Drop a crash bag (canvas or muslin sack holding tin, glass, rocks, etc.), or try a thunder sheet or kettledrum.

The light man's contribution to the play is significant. He helps JEN tell her story by shifting illumination from the apron to the main set. Arrange lights for the apron that can be controlled apart from the living room's. See the Guide.

As always, there is much latitude in arriving at lighting effects. Experimenting is in order. Highly recommended: a light rehearsal or two.

Publicity

She Loves Him Yes extols self-expression. That theme can spark a lively publicity campaign!

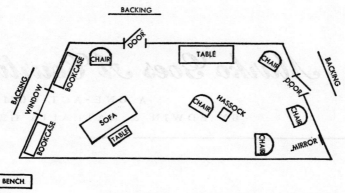

GROUND PLAN

FURNISHINGS		PROPERTIES
bench	portfolio	paper
sofa	table runners	pencil
coffee table	tablecloth	cookies and nuts
table	flowers	silverware
hassock	flower bowl	napkins
mirror	tray	tea sandwiches
chairs	dishes	jug of cider
lamps	glasses	scrubbing brush
end tables	two platters of	sponge
bookcases	doughnuts	large mixing bowl
	book	skillet
	fruit and popcorn	shirts
	writing board	

Marko Goes A Courtin'

A ONE-ACT COMEDY
BY EDWIN & NATHALIE GROSS

Cast of Characters

Campers of West-2
(in early teens)

PAT WILLS	Junior Group President, capable and popular.
RUTH	timid and law-abiding.
JINGO	overweight, good-natured, roguish, exuberant.
LUCY	pretty, a bit sophisticated.

Counselors
(college age)

STELLA	in charge of West-2 and campus night watch. Somewhat serious and reserved.
CIBBY	in charge of another Junior bungalow and assistant night watch. Relaxed and well-liked.

PLACE: Junior bungalow West-2 at Camp Papago.

TIME: Shortly before bedtime during the second week of camp.

The scene is the interior of bungalow West-2 at Camp Papago, a girls' summer camp. Down right is the entrance from campus. This door remains open throughout, admitting moonlight. The bunk light switch is near it. A door to the washroom is up left.

The one window needed is up center. Five cots are along the walls: two at stage right (STELLA'S, near the entrance, and RUTH'S, further upstage), one up center (PAT'S), one up left (LUCY'S), and one down left (JINGO'S). There are five trunks, one by each cot. Clothing, pennants, photographs, sports equipment, odd signs, a posted duty roster, and assorted personal effects are in evidence. The center of the bunk is free of furnishings.

It is shortly before bedtime during the second week of camp.

The curtain rises on PAT, RUTH and JINGO. PAT, in bathrobe, pajamas, and slippers, sits on her trunk writing a letter and swatting at an occasional mosquito. RUTH, in pajamas and bathrobe, sits on her cot massaging a sprained ankle with liniment. JINGO, in pajamas, lies flat on her back at center. She is doing bicycle exercises half-heartedly. She stops.

JINGO: Lovely moon, you know?

RUTH: Nothing special.

JINGO: It's like a big Gouda cheese hanging over the campus. Makes me hungry. [*Exercises briefly, halts.*]

RUTH: Pat?

PAT: Hmmm?

RUTH: Try some of Lucy's mosquito lotion.

PAT: Good idea. [*Crosses, applies lotion from bottle near LUCY'S cot.*]

RUTH: How's your letter going?

PAT: Pretty slow. I never know what to say to my aunts.

JINGO: Wish you'd make a copy for me.

RUTH: But you don't do half the things Pat does. What did you tell them?

PAT: Oh, you know. Same girls in my bunk again but a brand new counselor. [*Returns to trunk.*]

JINGO: Who stinks!

PAT: And my nature exhibit is flourishing. And then about the Junior dance this Saturday night. . . .

RUTH: Did you mention being elected Junior President? Twenty in the group, and you're *it!*

JINGO: Sure—make it tough for your cousins.

PAT: [*Modestly*] Oh, Mom's probably spread the word.

JINGO: [*Sighing*] Ah me, back to the daily dozen! [*Exercising*] Does exercise really take off weight? [LUCY *enters from washroom in modish matching robe and pajamas, hair in pincurls. She is peering into a hand mirror.*]

LUCY: I'm so sunburned I feel like a cactus. Keep it up, Jingo. It can't hurt. [*Sits on cot, pats hair expertly, then concentrates on painting toenails.*]

JINGO: Hurt! I ache all over! More of this and I won't be able to dance a step Saturday. [*Glumly*] If anyone asks me to dance. [*Rises. Donning robe and slippers*] I read once about a genius. Got all his exercise winding his watch once a day. Pretty should be all a girl needs. [*Sits, pulls a violin case from under her cot and takes a candy box from it. Eating candy*] And another layer bit the dust! [*Emptying cardboard between layers and excess wrappers onto bed*] Wouldn't I howl if this box had a false bottom. [*Offering candy*] How's the sprained ankle, Ruthie?

RUTH: [*Taking piece*] Pretty fair. Gives me an excuse if I'm a wallflower Saturday. [JINGO *offers candy to* LUCY *and* PAT.]

LUCY: What's the matter, Ruthie, my gal? Where's the spirit of bunk West-2?

JINGO: Easy for you to talk, Lucy.

RUTH: [*Enviously*] You're a wonderful dancer.

PAT: [*Slipping letter into envelope*] Oh, well, I'm sure we'll all have a swell time. . . .

JINGO: [*Sarcastically*] If our beloved counselor isn't made chaperone. [*Puts candy back in violin case, shoves it under bed.*]

LUCY: She thinks this is a reformatory. Never a compliment, never any fun.

JINGO: All I need to finish off the dance is Stella's eye on me. Boy, when she gets on her high horse! [*Perches sunglasses on tip of nose. Mimicking old-fashioned schoolmarm*] Jingo, is your bed ready for a surprise inspection? Ruth, up tall, girl, don't slouch. Lucy, remember, no couples leave the social hall. Pat Wills—where's Pat? Anyone here seen Pat?

PAT: [*Playing along, coyly stepping forward*] Here I am, Stella.

JINGO: [*Still pretending*] As President of the Juniors you must help me supervise this dance. This will identify you as head monitor. [*Pins sock on PAT'S robe.*] I'm counting on you.

PAT: [*Mock protest*] But Stella, this is the first chance to meet the Junior boys——

JINGO: [*Snapping*] Pat Wills, I am the joy killer—oops, I mean the chaperone here! Do as I say!

PAT: Yes, Stella.

JINGO: [*Retiring to cot*] Gee-ronimo! Some pet peeve we're stuck with! And the season only one week old! [PAT *returns to her cot, removing sock. She starts brushing a pair of shoes.*]

LUCY: My fourth summer at Camp Papago and I have to meet up with her!

JINGO: My fifth—and she's ruining it!

RUTH: [*Moved to protest, timidly loyal*] Oh, Jingo, you love to exaggerate. Stella's not so bad.

JINGO: She sure hides her light under a—a toothpick.

RUTH: You don't understand her.

JINGO: Yeh?

RUTH: She's the best arts and crafts head Papago ever had.

JINGO: Where's her sense of humor? That's the most important thing. A counselor's s'posed to be one of us, and yet not one of us. She's just *not* one of us.

RUTH: Maybe she's homesick. She's never been to camp before.

LUCY: Pat, please ask the director to let *Cibby* chaperone the dance.

PAT: You bet.

LUCY: You should've been on the hike today, Ruthie. Stella's rules! No acorn fights, no wading, no cheering near the boys' camp. . . .

JINGO: Somebody ought to tell her what camp's all about. I made up a song. Want to hear?

PAT: Get it out of your system before "Taps."

JINGO: [*Clears throat. Singing to tune of "Tarantara, Tarantara" from "The Pirates of Penzance"*]

Oh, when Stella starts to nag,
Tarantara, tarantara!
Our good spirits swiftly flag,
Tarantara!

And we find the wisest thing,
>>Tarantara, **tarantara!**
Is to shut our ears and sing
>>Tarantara!
For what Stella's out to do. . . .

LUCY: [*Gasping*] Chickie!

JINGO: [*Switching to tune of "On Wisconsin," gesturing vigorously*]

>On Papago, on Papago,
>On to victory;
>To our colors high afloat
>We pledge our loyalty.
>Rah, rah, rah . . . !

[STELLA *enters from campus. Obviously tired, she wears glasses, shorts, and a blouse. A whistle and small megaphone are strung about her neck.*]

STELLA: What energy, Jingo.

JINGO: Maybe I'll make song leader yet. [LUCY *giggles.*]

STELLA: Jingo! Are those candy wrappers on your bed?

JINGO: [*Calmly*] Uh-huh.

STELLA: Shouldn't you go easy? You know what the doctor said. . . .

RUTH: She did her exercises already.

STELLA: [*Tensely*] Well. . . . How's the ankle, Ruthie?

RUTH: Better, thanks. I can walk on it.

STELLA: Check at the infirmary tomorrow, anyway. Everybody write a letter home?

PAT: Yes, Stella.

STELLA: Now let's see. [*Sighs.*] Lucy, did you sew on your swimming insignia?

LUCY: Yes, Stella.

STELLA: Pat, you do the play review for the newspaper?

PAT: Hours ago.

STELLA: Well, you're all toeing the mark tonight. That hike wore me out, too. [*Takes flashlight and sweater, which she slips on, from trunk.*] Almost time for lights out. Everybody ready?

LUCY: I still have one foot to do.

STELLA: I'm head campus watch tonight. I'll expect you girls to be extra good.

PAT: Who's your assistant watch?

STELLA: Cibby.

LUCY: She's cute.

STELLA: [*Relaxing on cot*] My head's splitting!

RUTH: Want an aspirin?

STELLA: I'd rather just have quiet.

JINGO: [*Spiritedly*] Excuse us for living!

STELLA: [*Realizing girls are upset*] Sorry. No reflection on you kids. I'm—I'm just not used to camp, I guess. [*Looks at watch, rises.*] Golly, it's late! [*Crosses to door to campus, blows whistle. Calling off through megaphone*] Midget lights out nowww! Warneeeng tooo Freshmen! [*To girls*] Remember, no noise after lights out. I don't want any trouble from my own bunk. [*Exits D.R.*]

JINGO: [*Huffily*] Her bunk! It's *our* bunk. She treats us like Freshmen!

RUTH: We upset her.

JINGO: What'd she think camp was? I'd like to enlighten her in a hurry.

PAT: [*Reflectively*] She really needs something. She's way off the beam now.

LUCY: Def.

JINGO: Boy, in the old days when campers had spirit, her bed would be pied!

LUCY: Oh, I don't know. Pie beds were talked about—but not made much.

JINGO: Baloney! It's a wonderful practical joke—it gets results! [*Excitedly*] Say, why don't we mess up her bed? Tonight!

LUCY: [*Singsonging*] Never get a good conduct pin that way.

JINGO: She'd blackball me, anyhow. And we'll all be in this together. Come on, Pat, what do you say?

PAT: Let me think about it.

JINGO: Look—it's perfect! She'll be out of the bunk long enough. . . .

RUTH: But she's tired and her head aches.

JINGO: Don't be a worry wart! Listen—we can't let her spoil the season for us.

LUCY: [*Giggling*] Remember *Macbeth*. "Well it were done quickly!"

JINGO: Right! I've a gorgeous idea! I know where there are some nice coily snakes. . . .

RUTH: You make me shiver.

PAT: Take it easy, Jingo. You're going overboard.

JINGO: Okay, how about some snails? No—a frog! Nothing wrong with a sweet li'l' jumpy frog!

PAT: [*Tempted*] A frog?

JINGO: Sure, that's what Stella needs! A frog in her bed! What do you say?

RUTH: I don't like it.

JINGO: Scaredy-cat!

RUTH: We're getting too old for such things.

JINGO: Oh—nimmity-pimmity!

LUCY: [*Considering*] It's not such a bad idea.

PAT: Has its points. I'm for it!

JINGO: [*Quickly*] Three against one; we do it! Zowie!

RUTH: [*Irresolutely*] I won't have to touch it, will I?

JINGO: No. Just don't tattle.

RUTH: Oh, I wouldn't!

LUCY: Tell me, please, where's this frog coming from?

JINGO: Why, around here someplace.

PAT: I'll catch it.

JINGO: You're best at that sort of thing, but I'll go if you don't want to.

PAT: I don't mind. [*Starts changing into sneakers.*]

JINGO: Good girl! Hot tamale! [*Rubs hands gleefully.*]

PAT: Cover up for me, if you have to.

JINGO: Oh, sure, sure.

RUTH: [*Limping to* PAT'S *cot*] Where are you going to look?

PAT: Down near the lake. I'll cut through the woods. [JINGO *looks out the door to the campus.* PAT *takes flashlight and moves to window.*]

JINGO: Coast is clear.

LUCY: [*Nervously*] Be careful and hurry back. Wait—a raincoat! [*Dashes to washroom. Returns with raincoat.*]

PAT: Thanks. [*Drops bathrobe on cot and puts on raincoat.*]

RUTH: This makes me jumpy.

JINGO: Like a frog. Joke! Good luck, Pat. [PAT *disappears through window.*]

RUTH: What if Stella comes in?

JINGO: Oh, I'll think of something.

LUCY: [*Laughing.*] Don't say you sent Pat for candy. [RUTH *limps back to cot. Whistle blows off on campus.*]

STELLA: [*Off*] Freshman lights out nowww! Warneeng tooo Sophomores!

JINGO: [*Reading duty roster*] Hey! Pat's down for sweep-up. We'll never pass bed-check inspection. Any volunteers?

RUTH: My ankle lets me out.

LUCY: Choose you, Jingo. Odds. Once takes it. [LUCY *and* JINGO *choose.*]

JINGO: I win. You do it. The broom's in the washroom. [LUCY *exits to washroom, returns immediately with broom and dustpan.*]

RUTH: I helped mind the Sophs today. Those kids have more energy!

LUCY: [Sweeping, eagerly] What's little Deedie Gordon like?

JINGO: It's her *brother* you're interested in—isn't it?

LUCY: [Casually] He's on my list.

JINGO: [Knowingly] On your *mind*.

RUTH: Well, Deedie's a brat. She kept saying: "You have to let me do whatever I want. My mother said so."

JINGO: I ought to be that kid's counselor a few days! [Smacks hands.]

LUCY: What are you wearing to the dance, Jingo?

JINGO: Navy slacks—for that long lean look—maybe.

RUTH: [To LUCY] I suppose your outfit'll overwhelm the stag line.

LUCY: If Mom sends my sequin blouse by Saturday.

JINGO: Sequin! Maybe *you* need a frog in your bed, pal.

LUCY: You're just not up on style.

JINGO: Style doesn't help me. Boys still want to be a brother to me.

RUTH: Wonder how Pat's making out.

JINGO: Me too. [Looking out window] No sign of her. If I'd gone I'd have hurried. [Holds dustpan for LUCY.]

LUCY: Listen, Flash, you'd fall in the lake or something. Remember the Treasure Hunt last year?

JINGO: My side won, didn't it? [Exits to washroom with broom and dustpan.]

RUTH: Over your wet body.

JINGO: [*Off*] Never heard me complain. [*Returning to her cot*] Say, why doesn't Stella date any counselors in the boys' camp? Ever figured that one out?

LUCY: [*Cattily*] I have a personal theory——

RUTH: [*Thoughtfully*] She wears a locket——

JINGO: Probably left over from childhood. [*Whistle blows off on campus.*]

STELLA: [*Off, nearby*] Sophomore lights out nowww! Warneeng tooo Intermediates! [JINGO *crosses and peers out door to campus.*]

JINGO: [*Softly*] Stella's coming! [*Strides to window and stands guard.*]

LUCY: Pat's robe! [*Dashes to* PAT'S *cot and sits on robe, concealing it.* STELLA *and* CIBBY *enter R.*]

STELLA: Those Freshmen're impossible. What a night!

CIBBY: You're just overtired, Stel. Hi, girls!

GIRLS: Hi, Cibby.

STELLA: Sweeping done?

JINGO: Yep.

STELLA: [*Casually*] Where's Pat?

JINGO: [*Matter-of-factly*] Oh, somewhere around.

STELLA: Better be here for lights out. [*Reaches in trunk.*] Here's my address book, Cib. You'll find it under "W."

CIBBY: Right. [STELLA *exits to washroom.* CIBBY *sits on* STELLA'S *cot.*] Got any paper, Lucy? And a pencil?

RUTH: [*Quickly*] Here, Cibby.

CIBBY: Thanks. [*Consults book and writes. Chuckling*] I'd do this in shorthand—but it would take me longer. [*Girls laugh.* STELLA *reenters.*] How do you feel, Stel?

STELLA: I took two aspirins.

CIBBY: You know, Stel, you shouldn't stand watch tonight at all. I can handle our shifts alone. [JINGO *and* LUCY *trade worried looks.*]

STELLA: Thanks, Cibby. But it wouldn't be fair.

CIBBY: [*Laying down book*] Really, Stel, I don't mind.

STELLA: I hate to walk out on a job.

CIBBY: Well, you'll go off early—you can count on that.

STELLA: We'll see. Be good, girls. Good night.

CIBBY: [*Smiling, returning pencil to* RUTH] Obstinate, isn't she? [*Waving*] Sleep tight, kittens. Good night.

GIRLS: Good night. [STELLA *and* CIBBY *exeunt D.R.*]

LUCY: [*Slipping* PAT'S *bathrobe under her pillow*] That was easy. [*Returns to her cot.*]

JINGO: [*Leaving window*] Wish I was in Cibby's bunk.

LUCY: She's a honey.

JINGO: Sure, a real old Papagoer. *She* knows the ropes around here.

LUCY: Hope I can be as poised when I'm a counselor.

RUTH: Stella's two years ahead in college and has a scholarship——

JINGO: [*Scoffingly*] Stella!

RUTH: Funny Cibby seems to like her.

JINGO: She doesn't have to live with her.

PAT: [*Softly, appearing at window*] Hellooo!

LUCY: [*Gasping*] Oh!

RUTH: Pat!

JINGO: [*Crossing to window*] Got a frog?

PAT: Here. [*Passes it carefully to* JINGO. *Climbing through window*] Isn't he a beauty? [*Removes raincoat.*]

RUTH: Keep him away from me!

JINGO: [*Cooing to frog*] Hello. Hello, honey. [*To* PAT] Stel and Cibby just left. [LUCY *throws* PAT *her bathrobe, takes raincoat to washroom.*]

PAT: I know. I heard them. Almost smothered Marko. Didn't want him to beep. [*Sits on cot and removes sneakers.*]

JINGO: So your name's Marko!

LUCY: [*Returning*] Christened already?

PAT: Yep. After Mark Twain. He made jumping frogs famous.

JINGO: Fat little fellow.

RUTH: Don't let that thing loose. He makes me jittery.

JINGO: Marko wouldn't hurt you. Would you, honey? Speak to my friend, Marko. [*Shrugs.*] Perverse.

PAT: Come on, Jingo. [*Crosses with* JINGO *to* STELLA'S *cot.*] Lucy, keep lookout. [LUCY *stands near door to campus.*]

RUTH: [*Limps to* STELLA'S *cot. Pleading*] Look. Let's not put the frog in Stella's bed.

JINGO: [*Snapping*] You tetched?

Marko Goes a Courtin' • **193**

RUTH: [*Doggedly*] Put him in her trunk. It's not so repulsive.

JINGO: No.

RUTH: I hate to think of that—that squiggly thing between anybody's sheets!

JINGO: Ye gods!

PAT: Calm down, Jingo. Ruthie's right. We'll put him in her pillowcase.

RUTH: That's better. [*Limps back to her cot. Whistle blows off on campus.*]

STELLA: [*Off*] Intermediate lights out nowww! Warneeng tooo Juniors!

PAT: Let's hurry.

JINGO: Here you go, my li'l' old palsy. [*Releasing frog inside pillowcase*] Frighten Stella and make her jump. [*Peering into case*] Settle down now. Ker-flop, ker-plop, ker-plunk! Good boy! [*Knotting open end of case*] And some strong knots! There!

LUCY: Her pajamas are sticking out.

JINGO: Uh-uh. [*Shoves pajamas under pillow, smooths it.*]

RUTH: You'd better wash your hands.

PAT: Afraid of warts? Superstition!

JINGO: [*Smacking hands*] How hard'll Stella hit the ceiling when she finds Marko? That is the question.

LUCY: [*Returning to her cot*] Well, we'll be sleeping. It's her problem, not ours.

JINGO: Very considerate frog. Quiet. Did he have a voice when you met him?

PAT: Strictly bass. Trr-r-r-onk, trr-r-r-onk, trr-r-r-onk.

JINGO: I thought frogs said "jug o' rum."

PAT: Not this one. Stella miss me?

JINGO: Not much.

PAT: Who swept?

LUCY: I did.

PAT: Thanks. I'm chilly. [*Removes robe and crawls under blankets.*] Snap out the light soon as Stella calls.

JINGO: Okay. She'll think we're sick.

RUTH: Hope Marko's family doesn't come looking for him. [*Takes off robe and climbs into bed. JINGO peeks out door to campus, then waits by light switch. LUCY kneels, prays silently, removes robe, and climbs into bed. Whistle blows off on campus.*]

STELLA: [*Off*] Junior lights out nowww! Warneeng tooo Seniors!

JINGO: [*Flicking off bunk light*] Sweet dreams, gang. Don't let the froggies bite! [*Takes off robe and slippers and climbs into bed. Moonlight streams in through the door. Voices are low through the next scene. Pause.*]

RUTH: [*Snapping on flash*] Think I'll read under the covers. I don't feel sleepy. [*Takes book from trunk, reads.*]

JINGO: Can a frog bite his way through a pillowcase?

LUCY: We'll find out soon.

RUTH: [*Half earnestly*] Got an extra flash, somebody? I'm staying up all night. [*Pause*]

JINGO: Ruthie.

RUTH: What?

JINGO: If you were a ghost, you'd be afraid of people. Joke! [*Pause. Singing folksong*]

> Oh, the frog went a courtin' and he did ride,
> um-hum, um-hum,
> Oh, the frog went a courtin' and he did ride
> With a sword and pistol by his side. . . .

LUCY: Shh! [*Pause. Calling softly*] Pat! You awake?

PAT: Yes.

LUCY: I've been thinking—this frog business. Isn't it—er—kind of petty? Makes me feel silly.

PAT: I've been thinking, too. It *is* juvenile.

JINGO: [*Defensively*] Hey!

RUTH: I've been against the whole thing. All along.

PAT: [*Sitting up*] Listen. How about letting the frog go?

JINGO: [*Sitting up*] What a bunch of softies!

LUCY: [*Sitting up*] Three against one, Jingo!

PAT: [*Rising*] It's no crime to change your mind. [*Crossing to* STELLA'S *cot*] We'll think of something better. Less crude. Better douse your flash, Ruthie. [RUTH *flicks off flash and sits up. Whistle blows off on campus.*]

STELLA: [*Off*] Senior lights out nowww! Good night, everybody! [LUCY *springs up and crosses to door D.R.*]

PAT: Where is she?

LUCY: Near the flagpole. [PAT *starts untying knots in* STELLA'S *pillowcase. A bugle blows "Taps" off in the distance.*]

PAT: I'll let Marko out the window. What knots!

JINGO: [*Rising, grudgingly*] Oh, all right, I'll help.

PAT: Swell. [JINGO *and* PAT *untie knots. Lifting out frog*] Nice Marko. Don't be nervous, fellow.

RUTH: Junk him!

PAT: [*Playfully*] It's really a shame to turn you out into the cold. Want to say good-by to the girls? [*Approaching* RUTH] Start with Ruthie.

RUTH: [*Nervously*] Pat, don't you dare!

PAT: [*Teasingly*] After all, Ruth, if you ever take Biology lab. . . .

RUTH: We'll discuss that some other time.

PAT: As you say. [*Stumbles against* RUTH'S *trunk. Dismayed*] Yikes! I lost him!

JINGO: Butterfingers!

LUCY: Pat Wills!

RUTH: [*Scared*] Where'd he go?

PAT: I don't know!

JINGO: [*Chuckling*] He's over near you, Ruthie!

RUTH: [*Terrified*] No!

JINGO: He just hopped under your blanket!

PAT: Stop it, Jingo!

JINGO: Well, I saw. . . .

RUTH: [*Shrilly*] I feel something! [*Shrieks, hops out of bed.*]

LUCY: Hush up!

RUTH: [*Screaming*] He's on me, he's on me!

JINGO: [*Laughing*] Don't be a sap! [*Whistle blows off on campus.*]

STELLA: [*Off, calling*] What's the noise, West-2?

LUCY: Stella!

PAT: Jingo—you clown!

JINGO: You started it!

PAT: Back to bed, everybody!

LUCY: Here she comes! [PAT, JINGO, *and* LUCY *scurry under covers.*]

JINGO: Ruthie, relax! I didn't really see him.

RUTH: [*Gingerly sitting on cot*] Well, where is he? [STELLA *enters from campus.*]

STELLA: [*Shining flashlight around*] What's going on here? [*No answer*] What was all the fuss? I'm waiting! [*No answer*] Ruth? [JINGO *giggles.*] Pat?

PAT: I'm—I'm afraid I can't tell you.

STELLA: The only noise on campus—and it's *my* bunk! I'm ashamed of you! [*With controlled anger*] You girls have been obedient the last couple of days. Now you're having a relapse. Well, it'll end right now. [*Flicking on bunk light*] All of you—out of bed! [PAT, JINGO, *and* LUCY *rise.*] You're no exception, Ruthie! [RUTH *rises.*] Robes and slippers. [*Girls don them.*] Now line up facing me. [*Girls,* RUTH *limping, take positions side by side at C.*] We'll see if exercise can make you sleepy.

JINGO: It always wakes me up. [JINGO *and* LUCY *titter.*]

RUTH: What about my ankle?

STELLA: Move only your arms.

JINGO: This makes my daily two-dozen.

STELLA: [*Frostily*] 'Tention! Wipe those smiles off. [*Girls pass hands over mouths.*] Throw them down. [*Girls gesture.*] Stamp on them. Go on! [*Girls except* RUTH *stamp.*] All right —hands on hips. Now: touching toes, and back to hips. Quickly. Let's go! [*As girls exercise*] One—two. One—two. One. . . . All the way down, Jingo. Keep your knees straight. . . . Two!

CIBBY: [*Appearing in doorway to campus*] What's the trouble, Stel?

STELLA: They won't say. And I'm fed up. Let's go, girls. One—two. One—two. We'll try some arm rotation. Ready? In time. Roll, two, three, four. Back, two, three, four. [CIBBY *strolls to* JINGO *and gently straightens her arms.* STELLA *counts on several times.*] All right. Back to bed. [*Girls climb into bed,* RUTH *cautiously.*] Any more noise and we'll repeat the performance. [*Flicking off light*] Good night. Come, Cibby. [*Exits to campus with* CIBBY. *Girls' voices are subdued.*]

RUTH: [*Fuming*] Of all the nerve!

JINGO: [*Springing from bed*] Hazing like that!

RUTH: Like to complain to the director!

PAT: It was corny, all right.

LUCY: In front of Cibby—that's what I minded. [*Sits up.*]

JINGO: I'm glad I snickered right at her. [*Remembering*] Say, where's Marko?

RUTH: [*Flicking on flash*] Find him! You have to!

JINGO: We were right before. He belongs in Stella's pillow. [*Sidles to door to campus and peeks out.*]

LUCY: It was stupid to take him out.

PAT: [*Rising*] I'll look for him.

JINGO: Wish he were twins. Chickie! [*Girls scramble under covers.* RUTH *snaps off flash.* STELLA *appears in doorway D.R.*]

STELLA: [*Shining flash around*] I'm glad you're quiet. [*Disappears. Pause*]

JINGO: A policeman!

PAT: [*Rising*] No noise now. Jingo, you be lookout. [JINGO *rises, stands guard near door.* PAT *takes her flash, shields it with handkerchief, and searches.* LUCY *and* RUTH *sit up.*]

JINGO: She's across campus. With Cibby. [*Singing softly*]

> Oh, dear Marko, where are you?
>> Tarantara, tarantara!
> In a corner or a shoe,
>> Tarantara.
> Please come out as fast you can,
>> Tarantara, tarantara. . . .

PAT: I see him!

RUTH: Thank goodness!

PAT: [*Creeping under* LUCY'S *cot*] Here, Marko!

JINGO: That girl attracts everything—even frogs.

PAT: Got him!

JINGO: Cibby's coming! [PAT *flicks off flash, starts toward cot.*] Unh-unh, false alarm.

PAT: [*Crossing to* STELLA'S *cot*] Let's get this over with. [*Putting frog in pillowcase*] Inside, Marko. [*Knots case.*]

RUTH: I'm not crazy about doing it, but I don't really object.

LUCY: Knot it any old way.

PAT: Yep. There! [*Returns to her cot, climbs under covers.*]

JINGO: [*Returning to cot*] When Stella finds him—I'd like to see her face!

LUCY: Maybe she'll wake us up for more exercises.

JINGO: [*Climbing under covers*] No. She won't want it to get around her own bunk pied her bed. With a frog, no less.

PAT: Settle down, everybody. [RUTH *and* LUCY *lie down.*]

JINGO: Won't it be awful if she's so tired she doesn't feel Marko?

LUCY: Well, her pajamas are under the pillow. . . .

PAT: Go to sleep. [*Pause*]

JINGO: [*Singing softly*]

Oh, the frog went a courtin' and he did ride, um-hum, um-hum. . . .

PAT: Pipe down. [*Pause*]

RUTH: Wonder what time it is.

LUCY: Stella doesn't come off duty for hours.

JINGO: Ever hear the one about the elevator man? He got so tired of people asking what time it was. . . .

PAT: You told that one the other day. Now let's not spoil everything. Keep quiet.

JINGO: Silence in the courthouse the monkey wants to speak! [*Pause.* STELLA *and* CIBBY *enter from campus, speaking softly.*]

STELLA: Feel like a heel turning in early.

CIBBY: I insist, Stel. You'll be fine in the morning.

STELLA: I do appreciate it, Cib.

CIBBY: Forget it. The hard part's over—campus is quiet. Bed-check won't take long.

STELLA: If you need me, call.

CIBBY: [*Lightly*] Okay. If there's a crisis.

STELLA: I'll stand your watch any night you want.

CIBBY: I'll hold you to that. Good night, Stel.

STELLA: Good night. [CIBBY *exits D.R.* STELLA *sits on her cot, sighs and looks around. She rises, lights her flash, and checks each cot, straightening* RUTH'S *blankets and unfolding* LUCY'S *spare one over her. She returns to her cot, briefly studies contents of a locket around her neck, then exits to the washroom.* LUCY *cautiously rises on one elbow and waves to* JINGO. JINGO *raises clasped hands like a triumphant prize fighter, strokes her pillow, raises hands again, settles down.* STELLA *returns and reaches under her pillow. Alarmed, she pokes it exploringly, then tries to pull off the case. Shocked*] It's knotted! [*Trying to open knots*] It's—it's—it's—ohh! [*Sinks face down on cot, sobbing softly. Brief pause. The girls, one by one, sit up self-consciously.*]

JINGO: Gee-ronimo!

LUCY: [*Clears throat.*] What'll we do?

JINGO: I don't know. I didn't expect this.

RUTH: She feels horrible. And so do I. [PAT *rises and flicks on bunk light.*] Poor Stella! [STELLA *curbs sobbing but remains face down.*]

PAT: [*Gently*] May I take your pillow, Stella? [*No answer.* PAT *takes pillow and exits D.R.*]

RUTH: [*Miserably*] Don't cry. Please. [LUCY *crosses to* JINGO. PAT *returns and lays pillow and empty case on* STELLA'S *cot.*]

PAT: [*Resting hand shyly on her shoulder*] We owe you an apology, Stel.

STELLA: [*Tearfully*] Never mind.

LUCY: [*Softly*] Kills me to see anybody cry.

JINGO: I can't take it either.

PAT: Ah, Stel, we're a bunch of simps. Don't let us get you down.

STELLA: [*Sitting up, with more control now*] Sorry to make a scene. Excuse me, girls. [*Wipes eyes with handkerchief.*]

PAT: We pulled a nasty trick—that's what.

STELLA: [*Slowly, with resignation*] With the whole bunk against me—I might as well. . . .

RUTH: [*Limping to* STELLA'S *trunk*] Oh, we're not really against you, Stel.

PAT: Course not—only. . . .

STELLA: I know, I'm a failure as your counselor. . . .

PAT: [*Quickly*] I wouldn't say that. Gosh, Stel, camp's—well—camp makes us want to be wacky—a bit. Not bad—or mean —but—well—campy. And you. . . .

STELLA: You don't help a newcomer get the hang. . . .

RUTH: [*Stanchly*] Stella's right. My first year I put in two weeks writing Dad to take me home.

STELLA: [*Ruefully*] I'm a little old for that—or I'd try it.

JINGO: [*Sincerely*] Don't quit, Stella. You could be a swell counselor—if you'd relax some—take things easier—like me. [*Impulsively*] Here, have some candy. [*Producing box from violin case*] I won't take advantage of you. [*Helping self*] Only one piece for me. [*Passes box to* STELLA.]

STELLA: [*Instinctively*] Oh Jingo, how'll you ever reduce—[*Grins, changing tack.*] You know that speech as well as I do. [*Taking piece*] Thanks.

JINGO: That's a good sport.

STELLA: Mmm, delicious. Now there are two of us'll have to show self-control. [*Girls chuckle.* JINGO *offers candy around.*]

LUCY: Guess we've made it rough, Stel. But you really invited it. [*Crosses and sits on* STELLA'S *cot.*]

PAT: [*Half jokingly*] Your memory for rules is remarkable.

JINGO: I never could bear nagging. Makes me want to disobey.

STELLA: Can't have you rebelling by eating candy. There'll be none left for me. [*Girls chuckle again.*] Reminds me of my first puppy. I was too strict with him till a neighbor showed me how to—to handle him.

PAT: [*Smiling*] Are we like the puppy—or the neighbor?

STELLA: [*Thoughtfully*] A bit of both. [*Confidingly*] Do you girls think you can keep a secret?

RUTH: Oh, yes.

JINGO: Sure!

STELLA: It definitely mustn't leak out.

PAT: We promise.

STELLA: Well, I'm engaged to that neighbor. We haven't announced it yet—for family reasons.

JINGO: [*Excited*] Wow! That's romantic! What's his name?

STELLA: Doug. And he lives right across the street from me.

LUCY: No wonder you don't date Papago men!

RUTH: When's the wedding?

STELLA: Probably next summer.

PAT: [*Mock despair*] You mean all our work's just for one season?

STELLA: [*Jokingly*] I could postpone the date. . . .

LUCY: Down with Patsy!

STELLA: Would you like to see Doug's picture?

LUCY: You bet!

JINGO: And how!

STELLA: There's a tiny one in my locket. But I have a bigger one. Excuse me. [RUTH *rises.* STELLA *draws a large photograph from bottom of trunk. The girls crowd around.* PAT *whistles admiringly.*]

LUCY: He's slick!

JINGO: Imagine living near that! Need a flower girl for the wedding? [*Capers around, strewing imaginary petals from candy box and humming "Oh Promise Me."*]

STELLA: Shh! Lower!

PAT: [*Softly*] We'll have Cibby down on us.

LUCY: Pat. [*Beckons* PAT *off to one side. They whisper together.*]

RUTH: [*Shyly*] Stella—I feel I ought to apologize on my own behalf for that frog.

STELLA: Oh, that's what it was! I wasn't sure.

JINGO: He was a beaut. We named him Marko. Very fat and cuddly.

RUTH: Very repulsive you mean. Rrrr!

JINGO: Well, I guess it's all the way you happen to look at it.

PAT: [*Approaching with* LUCY] Stel—uh—we feel like jerks. Really. Please forget tonight—I mean the bad part and—uh —we'd like you to take charge of our dance Saturday. I can ask the director.

JINGO: That's a great idea! Stel, what do you say?

STELLA: Thank you, gang. I'd love to help.

PAT: Settled.

LUCY: Got any ideas for decorating?

JINGO: [*Jubilantly*] Arts and crafts counselor!

STELLA: Let's sleep on it. We'll compare notes in the morning. [*Gently*] Scoot to bed, kids.

PAT: Okay, Stel. Good night.

JINGO: Night.

LUCY: Night.

STELLA: Good night. [JINGO *puts candy box back in violin case.* PAT *and* LUCY *climb into bed.* STELLA *gets fresh pillowcase from trunk.*]

RUTH: [*Lingering*] Sleep tight, Stella. Get a good rest.

CIBBY: [*Appearing in doorway D.R.*] Everything under control here, Stel?

STELLA: Yes, Cibby.

CIBBY: [*Entering*] How's the headache?

STELLA: All gone!

CIBBY: Good! Look at this frog I found outside the bunk. [JINGO *runs over.*] Isn't he tremendous?

JINGO: [*Exclaiming*] It's Marko!

CIBBY: He sure is a twitchy little thing. [*Stumbles against* STELLA'S *trunk. Dropping frog near* RUTH] Oops! He got away! [RUTH *shrieks in terror.*]

The Curtain Falls.

NOTES ON STAGING

MARKO Goes a Courtin' is a natural for girls' schools, clubs, camps. There is a small cast and nary a male. Many age levels can produce it. Best of all, it inspires unity and good-will.

If you do the play at camp, work in local color. Recommended: your way of calling "Lights out," your group divisions, emblems, song.

A word on curtain calls. *Marko* ends on a note of laughter. More can be snared by amusing pantomimes. For example: (a) have the whole cast down on its knees hunting MARKO except RUTH who stands quaking on her cot, (b) have STELLA hold up MARKO triumphantly as RUTH flees in terror.

Acting

The camper quartet should take care to play well together; few people know each other like bunkmates. By picking up cues alertly and naturally, they will heighten suspense.

The four are rather defined types. PAT is a leader, confident, capable, fair-minded. RUTH is timid, somewhat prissyish. Keep her distaste for frogs believable. A sprained ankle makes her limp —slightly.

JINGO is breezy, exuberant, loves mischief. LUCY the most sophisticated, preens but is graceful and good fun.

The counselors should seem older, more reserved. STELLA is a worrier, very conscious of responsibility. And tonight she is tuckered out. CIBBY is a relaxed, cheerful old-timer.

When voices go low, aim for a hushed quality—but project to the back rows. Show-stopper Will Rogers used to drawl, "Our audiences are our best friends." They will not be if they cannot hear!

On the music: JINGO's "Tarantara" ditty is from Gilbert and Sullivan's operetta, *The Pirates of Penzance*. "On Wisconsin" is the familiar University of Wisconsin march. "The Frog Went a Courtin' " is in many folksong collections. "Oh Promise Me" from the operetta *Robin Hood* (and now traditional at weddings), is a stand-by in music albums.

Scenery and Furnishings

Marko's setting, the interior of a camp bungalow, is readily assembled. It calls for five cots and trunks, two exits, one window.

For the bunk's walls use flats, drapes and/or screens (see Guide).

Suggest a balance of clutter and tidiness that says, "Five active girls live here. Oops! They undergo daily inspection." Belongings and mementos are everywhere, yet their bunk is relatively neat.

The washroom exit can be, instead of a door, a portiered opening—that is, a doorway with curtains hanging across. The exit to campus, which is never closed, does not have to be practical.

PAT climbs through the window. Make that unit sturdy!

Use backing, if needed, at the campus door and window. Foliage is most appropriate.

Properties

MARKO, the frog, is the only uncommon prop. (Avoid realism here!) Use a toy that will not clank or break when dropped. Or mold MARKO from papier-mâché.

Get comedy from the signs around the bunk. You know—"Danger—Men Working," "No Trespassing," "Stop," "Do Not Disturb," etc.

Do not forget about testing flashlights before each performance.

Costumes and Make-up

Vary campers' pajamas and bathrobes. Be conservative if you are playing before wolf-callers or easy gigglers.

Pad JINGO subtly if nature has not. She is a bit overweight.

STELLA'S clothes should look new, not "part" of her. Her shorts can be just a speck long (the laundry has not shrunk them yet!), her blouse strictly regulation. CIBBY wears camp togs with a flair. She can personalize with a scarf, belt, etc.

The campers, bound for bed, wear discreet make-up suggesting well-scrubbed, sunburned skin. The counselors' make-up is more obvious.

Special Effects and Lighting

For "Taps," try a record or good bugler. Warning: bugles are loud! Check volume. Your bugler may have to stand outside the building.

STELLA'S whistle blasts might well come from different off-stage positions to show she is making her rounds on campus.

Be smooth with light cues. Rehearse. Do not trust to luck.

Even when bunk lights black out, keep on enough general illumination (see section on Lighting in Guide) to reveal the actors clearly. "Moonlight" and flashlights are the excuse for having any light at all. But in the theater they need help!

Once the effect of dimness is put across, sneak up more light gradually. It is normal stage practice. An audience does not question, accepting the idea that it is getting used to the dark.

For moonlight, try daylight blue or blue-green sheets of gelatin or cellophane over a spot. Or work with colored bulbs.

Publicity

Program editor, you can raise an extra chuckle by listing MARKO as played by "Himself."

Advertising for this show, which incidentally has won a national prize, can easily go imaginative. Be mysterious about, make much of MARKO. "Who is MARKO???" "Come see MARKO excel himself!" "Watch for The Green Hero!"

Possible captions for gag photos or cartoons: "The Timid One!" "Gang Leader!" "The Sophisticate!" "The Mischief Brewer!" "The Careworn Counselor!" Carry on.

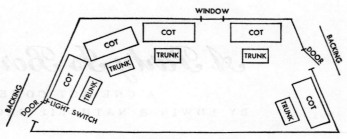

GROUND PLAN

FURNISHINGS	PROPERTIES	
five cots made up with blankets, sheets, pillows, and pillowcases five trunks	clothes	whistle
	pennants	small megaphone
	photographs	three flashlights
	sports equipment	sweater
	signs	sneakers
	duty roster	raincoat
	lotion bottle	broom
	PAT'S paper, pencil, envelope	dustpan
		address book
	hand mirror	LUCY'S paper and pencil
	nail polish	
	violin case	frog (imitation)
	candy box with candy, cardboard layer, and wrappers	book
		handkerchief
		LUCY'S spare blanket
		locket
	sunglasses	photograph (in STELLA'S trunk)
	sock	
	pin	pillowcase (in STELLA'S trunk)
	shoe brush	

A Party Is Born

A ONE-ACT COMEDY
BY EDWIN & NATHALIE GROSS

Cast of Characters

JANET LOSSING	vivacious, pretty, and just sixteen.
IRA LOSSING	her older brother, helpful but a bit patronizing.
MOM LOSSING	attractive, poised, in her early forties.
AUNT HELEN	coy, dowdy, about thirty-five.
RED O'NEIL	a jaunty neighbor about Ira's age.
YVONNE BARKLEY	sleek, affected, almost sixteen.
DAD LOSSING	jovial, pleasantly pompous, in his forties.
EILEEN	studious, bespectacled, fifteen.
PAUL CROWLEY	sedate, in his late teens.
DAVEY JENNINGS	smooth, ingratiating, in his late teens.

PLACE: Living room of the Lossing home.

TIME: Seven o'clock. The evening of JANET'S sweet-sixteen party.

The scene is the tastefully furnished living room of the LOSSING family. A sofa stands stage right. Up left, near the rear wall, is a piano bearing a vase, photo album, candy dishes, sheet music. On the floor, pinned securely under the piano, lies a large rug. Up

*center is a fireplace, up right center a window. A door to the din-
ing room is at left, a door to a hall at right. Both doors can remain open throughout. Chairs, end tables, lamps, bric-a-brac
complete the décor.*

*At the extreme down left and down right are two small areas
which light up only for telephone conversations. The one at right
shows the telephone nook in the* LOSSING *home. The one at left is
used to represent six different locales. Both contain a telephone on
a table and a chair.*

Shortly after the curtain rises JANET LOSSING, *in a formal gown,
enters R. with a framed portrait. It's seven o'clock on the evening
of her sweet-sixteen party. Except for some hair still in pincurls,
she is ready to greet her first guest.* JANET *sets her picture on the
fireplace mantel and backs away to appraise it. The front doorbell
rings.* JANET *sighs.*

JANET: If it isn't the telephone, it's the doorbell! [*Exits R., returns with florist's box, and unwraps it. She reads the card
and pins corsage on her gown. Calling*] Ira, come see!

IRA: [*Off L., calling*] Wait a minute, Jan.

JANET: It'll only take a second. [*Twirling*] I'm so excited I could
fly-y-y!

IRA: [*Entering L. in sport shirt and casual slacks*] Hey, Sis, you're
sweet sixteen! You're supposed to have dignity.

JANET: Dignity? What's that?

IRA: Why—that's what comes out at a coming-out party!

JANET: You can rib me—I'm immune tonight.

IRA: Oof, my aching palms! Three dozen bridge chairs I opened!

JANET: [*Bowing in mock humility*] Most sisterly thanks, oh supe-
rior brother!

A Party Is Born • 2 1 3

IRA: Skip it. Just remind me to skip town for your next brawl. [*Takes candy from piano.*]

JANET: Oh, you're enjoying the fuss. But everything has to be *right*. Yvonne Barkley's throwing a catered affair for her birthday.

IRA: Yvonne would. That hot-house bloom.

JANET: Like the corsage?

IRA: Ravishing, Miss Lossing. [*Sniffs.*]

JANET: Ninny, you don't smell corsages.

IRA: How should I know? No one's ever sent *me* one. Who's it from?

JANET: Mom and Dad.

IRA: I thought maybe that new guy on the block put himself out.

JANET: [*A bit breathlessly*] Davey Jennings? Don't be silly! He hardly knows I exist. I just invited him out of courtesy.

IRA: I guess he's coming 'cause he's heard about Grandma's potato salad.

JANET: Don't josh about poor Grandma or her salad.

IRA: Okay. [*Chuckling*] But when the old gal tripped and dumped the stuff all over the lawn———! Why'd she cook so much of it?

JANET: Grandma couldn't guess she'd sprain her ankle!

IRA: It's taking Mom forever to make her comfortable.

JANET: We're lucky. Everything's about ready, anyway. [*Moving to mantel*] Like my new portrait here?

IRA: [*Noncommittally*] Not bad.

JANET: Some help! Well, I'll ask Dad when he gets back.

IRA: If he'll speak to you after the shopping expedition you sent him on. Time's awastin'—I have to roll the rug. Then I can shower.

JANET: [*Startled*] Holy Hannah! I forgot about the rug!

IRA: You want it up, don't you?

JANET: Sure! This is the dance floor.

IRA: [*Surveying scene*] Now let's see. That piano—that's the only snag. It's got to be lifted. The rest of this furniture's a snap.

JANET: Whatever you say. Only *please* be careful.

IRA: Let's move this stuff away. [IRA *and* JANET *shift furniture off the rug. Phone off R. rings—and the small area D.R. is illuminated.*]

JANET: Uh-uh. I knew this peace couldn't last. I'll be right back, Ira. [*Exits R. as* IRA *sprawls on sofa.* JANET *appears at phone D.R. Into phone*] Hello. [*Light comes up on phone D.L., disclosing* MOM LOSSING.]

MOM: [*Into phone*] Hello, dear. How's everything coming along?

JANET: Just fine, Mom. Is Grandma feeling better?

MOM: Yes, but she'll have to stay off that ankle. Tell me, Janet, were the sandwiches delivered?

JANET: Uh-huh. And the carpenter fixed the Ping-pong table.

MOM: What about the maid? Has she phoned again?

JANET: Oh, yes. She'll be here in about an hour.

A Party Is Born • **215**

MOM: Darling, I'm so sorry I'm not home to help. Did Ira hang the lump sugar?

JANET: Yes. And his wisecracks about "sweet sixteen and never been kissed" were revolting!

MOM: Don't mind Ira, honey.

JANET: I'm not complaining, really. He's been wonderful. He did everything I asked. Blew up a million balloons for the dance —and pitched in everywhere.

MOM: How does the living room look, dear?

JANET: Just dandy, Mom. With the big rug out of the way it'll——

MOM: [*Surprised and annoyed*] The rug—the rug *what*, dear?

JANET: Taken up for dancing.

MOM: But, honey, you never made clear you'd take the rug up. You know it's very expensive. [IRA *rises, exits R. and appears behind* JANET.] Besides, the floor's just been scraped.

JANET: [*Wailing*] But dancing on the rug'd be awful!

MOM: [*Crisply*] No dramatics. You've done it plenty of times. Oh, dear—this *is* provoking.

JANET: [*Protesting*] Oh, Mom!

MOM: I don't quite know what to say. Well, I suppose if the rug's up—I might as well make the best of it. You didn't do any damage, did you?

JANET: [*Faintly*] No, course not. [*Softly to* IRA, *hand over mouthpiece*] Sst! Mom thinks the rug's up already!

MOM: Sorry I didn't call earlier! A neighbor's coming over to spend the night with Grandma. So I'll be home soon. Dad back yet? [IRA *reenters living room from R. He shifts remaining furniture off rug.*]

JANET: No, Mom. Give my love to Grandma.

MOM: Thank you, dear. See you in a little while.

JANET: 'Bye, Mom. [*Phones black out. Reentering living room from R.*] Ohh!

IRA: What's wrong, kid?

JANET: I put my foot in it! Why'd I let Mom think the rug was up?

IRA: Heck, it made sense. Remember *The Mikado*. If a thing's good as done why not say so?

JANET: [*Upset*] But it was practically a lie! Now if Mom comes home right away――――

IRA: [*Patronizingly*] Calm down, Sis. Gee whiz! You turning soft with age or something?

JANET: [*Sincerely*] Well, maybe these things don't matter to you —but they do to me.

IRA: [*Flippantly*] Okay, sweet sixteen, then let's get a move on. [*Gestures toward piano.*]

JANET: [*On her dignity*] You don't see it! If Mom finds out she'll think I fib whenever and wherever―――― You—you just don't understand our relationship!

IRA: Sounds like your course on Family Life. Why on earth do they give that stuff to high-school kids?

JANET: And I wanted this evening to be perfect!

IRA: [*Realizing need for speed*] All right, cut the chatter. We'll get everything straightened out.

JANET: But it's only twelve minutes by bus from Grandma's— and Mom might even taxi!

IRA: Hush yo' mouf, honey chile! [*Moves to piano, surveys it.*] First, clear away the junk. [JANET *removes sheet music, photo album, candy dishes, and vase, distributing them in room.*] Now I'll lift this ol' music box and you pull out the rug. [IRA *strains at one end of piano. He strains again. The piano doesn't budge. Ruefully*] No dice. Guess I can't handle it alone. This darn lame back. . . . [JANET *nods sympathetically.*] Suppose you give me a hand—and I'll kick the rug out.

JANET: Sure. Oh, Ira!

IRA: Save your breath, Sis. Come on! [JANET *and* IRA *take hold of piano. Front doorbell rings.*]

JANET: Glory be! 'Scuse me a sec. [*Exits R., reappears in doorway.*] Ira, lend me a dime.

IRA: Two nickels do? [*Passing her coins*] Who is it?

JANET: Telegram. [*Disappears R. Reentering quickly holding wire*] Wouldn't you know it? The Foster boys can't come.

IRA: Why not?

JANET: Doesn't say. It makes me sick! I had it all planned to have six more boys than girls. Why's it always the boys who back out?

IRA: No philosophy. We've got work. [*They return to piano. Phone D.R. rings and is illuminated.*] The house is haunted! Bells, bells, bells!

JANET: Be right back. [*Races off R. and appears at phone D.R. Light comes up on phone D.L., disclosing* AUNT HELEN. *She is coy, dowdy, about thirty-five. Into phone*] Hello?

AUNT HELEN: [*Into phone, singing*]

> Happy birthday to you!
> Happy birthday to you!
> Happy birthday, Janet Lossing,
> Happy birthday to you!

Did I fool you? Did you think it was Western Union?

JANET: Almost—Aunt Helen.

AUNT HELEN: Goodness me, I can't believe you're sixteen! How does it feel?

JANET: [*Impatiently*] Fine.

AUNT HELEN: I can remember *my* sixteenth birthday. I'll bet you're excited! Do you look glamorous?

JANET: Well, my hair's not all combed out. . . .

AUNT HELEN: Oh, g'wan, you must be beautiful. Is Mother there?

JANET: Not yet. Good-by. . . .

AUNT HELEN: I'd like Mother to phone me. . . .

JANET: I'll tell her. Good-by. . . .

AUNT HELEN [*Persevering*] Oh, by the way, dear, don't you want little Cousin Harriet to come tonight?

JANET: No, Aunt Helen! Er—only girls fifteen and over are invited. That's the rule.

AUNT HELEN: Your mother said something like that. But Harriet'd be so cute—and she could yodel—or recite—or——

JANET: [*Straining to be polite*] Thanks, Aunt Helen, but it wouldn't be fair to all the other cousins. Golly, I have to go now!

AUNT HELEN: Well, don't forget to have Mother phone me. Happy birthday! [*Phones black out.*]

JANET: [*Reentering living room from R.*] I could certainly do with fewer party-happy cousins and aunts!

IRA: Think you can concentrate on this job for two minutes?

JANET: [*Contritely*] Yes, Ira.

IRA: Well, grab hold. [JANET *gingerly grips piano.*] Bend down more.

JANET: [*Bends. Abruptly springing erect*] A run! My best pair! [*Licks finger, applies it to stocking.*]

IRA: [*Rasping*] Look, Sis, do we or do we not get this rug up before Mom comes home? No skin off my back, you know!

JANET: I'll change later. Let's go. [JANET *and* IRA *strain at piano unsuccessfully. Distraught*] It's no use! Oh, Ira, now everything *is* a mess!

IRA: [*Barking*] Quiet! [*Paces.* JANET *sits disconsolately on piano bench. Brightening*] I have it, kid. We'll call Red O'Neil.

JANET: No, he's a guest. It isn't etiquette.

IRA: Etiquette! Etiquette! Why the guy's known you all your life. He taught you how to ride a tricycle! [*Strides to window U.R. and whistles out. Shouting*] Hey, Red! [*Back doorbell buzzes.* JANET *exits L.*] Hey, Red!

RED: [*Off*] What do you want, Ira?

IRA: I need help. Domestic emergency. Can you come right over?

RED: [*Off*] I'm shaving.

IRA: Well, skip a few hairs.

RED: [*Off*] That's all I got.

IRA: [*Muttering*] A comedian. [*Calling*] We *need* you!

RED: [*Off*] Okay. Soon as I can.

IRA: [*Turning from window*] Etiquette! Hey, where are you, Janet?

JANET: [*Off*] Coming! [*Reenters L. wearing half-apron*] Bitsy Todd just came around the back. With extra ice cubes.

IRA: [*Jocularly*] His Nibs want to stay for the party?

JANET: I ignored the hints. I hate to be cruel to a nine-year-old.

IRA: He has a crush on you. Belle of the punchball team, that's you!

JANET: Don't joke. I'm getting shivers. If you catch me dreaming up another house party, kick me hard! I give you permission.

IRA: [*Soothingly*] Buck up, Sis. You'll stop counting your birthdays soon. [*Phone D.R. rings.*]

JANET: I could wring that phone's neck!

IRA: [*Jocularly*] Rrrip it out! [*JANET exits R. IRA sits at piano, looks through sheet music. Phone D.R. is illuminated.*]

JANET: [*Into phone*] Hello. [*Light comes up on phone D.L., disclosing YVONNE BARKLEY in dressing gown and facial pack. She is sleek, catty, affected.*]

YVONNE: [*Into phone. Archly*] This is Yvonne, Janney. Want me to come over and help?

JANET: [*Pretending composure*] Oh no, Yvonne. Everything's under control.

YVONNE: Good, I was only being polite. Frankly, I *hate* to rush before a party.

JANET: So do I.

YVONNE: I just had the most luxurious bubble bath. It always makes me feel so relaxed! [*Yawning elaborately*] Ohhh! Now I'm going to stretch out and nap.

JANET: [*Battling envy*] Bet you'll look swell.

YVONNE: My new gown's just precious! You'll never guess who sent my corsage!

JANET: [*In there fighting*] You'll never guess who sent mine!

YVONNE: Well, I suppose I'd better not keep you, Janney.

JANET: Oh, I've oceans of time, Yvonne. [*Sarcastically*] But I wouldn't want you to cut your beauty nap short. [*Purring*] 'Bye noww.

YVONNE: 'Bye, dearr. [*Phone D.L. blacks out.* JANET *thumbs nose at phone D.R. It blacks out.*]

JANET: [*Venomously, reentering R.*] Yvonne Barkley! Always queening about something.

IRA: [*Rising*] That li'l kid get in your hair again?

JANET: [*Removing apron*] Little kid, huh? [*Front doorbell rings. Tensely*] Oh my goodness! Maybe that's Mom!

IRA: Probably Red. [*Exits R. Off*] Why, Dad—here, let me help you! [*Reenters carrying loaded paper bags,* DAD LOSSING *following.* IRA *exits L.*]

JANET: [*Nervously*] Hi, Daddy.

DAD: Next time I go shopping for you I want a station wagon. [*Plumping down on sofa*] Pff! I'm fagged out. Know how many stores I was in? Neither do I; I couldn't count 'em! Janet, honey, we've cornered the market on chocolate-covered cherries. Our future's made! Like the flowers?

JANET: Oh, they're gorgeous, Daddy. You were sweet to send them.

DAD: Let me look at you, sugar. Kind of flushed, aren't you? [*Gently*] You ought to try to rest up. You'll enjoy the party more.

JANET: [*Nervously*] I'll try.

DAD: Anything good in the kitchen? [*Rising*] What've you been nibbling, Junior?

IRA: Sample the punch, Dad. And the Mexican pumpkin seeds.

DAD: Think I will. Before the locusts arrive. [*Exits L.*]

IRA: What do we do now, kid? You call the tune.

JANET: I'd better tell him. I—I *know* he'll fuss.

IRA: I'll tackle him with you. [*Calling*] Dad, can we see you please? [*Softly*] Least he's in a good mood.

DAD: [*Reentering L. with glass of punch and newspaper*] What is it? Heap big family powwow?

IRA: Sort of. You see, Dad, Janet has a problem.

DAD: Really? My Miss America? What's troubling you, hon?

JANET: [*Abashedly*] Well, Dad, you see—it's about this rug here. We'd like to roll it up for dancing.

DAD: [*Grandiosely*] Okay, roll it up!

IRA: Piano's in the way. We'll have to lift it first.

DAD: All right! [*Unburdens hands, flexes muscles.*] Lossing and Son, Piano Movers. Service With A Smile!

IRA: It's kind of heavy. I've called Red. He's going to help.

A Party Is Born • **223**

DAD: [*Rubbing hands*] Fine! I can supervise.

JANET: Er—one thing more. On the phone before Mom said—said she didn't want the rug up and—well—I guess I let her think we'd rolled it already. She'll be home any minute——

DAD: [*Thoughtfully*] Oh-ho.

JANET: If we don't hurry—and Mom sees I lied—it'll ruin everything!

DAD: [*Quietly*] What else did your mother have to say?

JANET: Oh, she asked if we'd done any damage getting it up . . . and if you were home. . . .

DAD: I see, I see. [*A strained pause. He motions toward sofa.* JANET *sits.*] Honey, first I want you to know I don't like your tactics. Honesty means a good deal to me . . . but for a very special occasion like this I'm going to make a *very special* exception. I'll go along with you tonight.

JANET: [*Much relieved*] Thanks, Dad.

DAD: [*Gruffly*] We'll discuss it more in the morning. There's *got* to be an accounting—the way I run things. [*In kinder vein*] I think we'd better hurry. [*Front doorbell sounds tattoo.*]

IRA: That's Red now. [*Exits R., returns with* RED O'NEIL. RED *is about* IRA'S *age. He wears a sweater, good trousers, and moccasins.*]

RED: Hello, everybody. Sorry I took so long.

JANET: Hi, Red.

RED: This entrance is strictly unofficial. I'll be back later with my new bow tie. Whoo-oo!

IRA: I can imagine.

DAD: Nice of you to come. We've a little job ahead that'll be pie with four of us. Let's see. How'll I handle this? [*Phone D.R. rings and is illuminated.*]

JANET: [*Exiting R.*] Oh, murder!

RED: Bet that phone's been singing all evening. Drives me crazy when my sister gives a party. Before *and* after! [JANET *appears at phone D.R. Light comes up on phone D.L., disclosing* EILEEN. *She is studious, bespectacled, about fifteen.* DAD, IRA *and* RED *exchange ideas sotto voce and finally reach agreement about handling the piano.*]

JANET: [*Into phone*] Hello.

EILEEN: [*Into phone. Timidly*] Hello? Janet?

JANET: Yes?

EILEEN: This is Eileen. I'm glad your brother didn't answer. I won't keep you—I know you're rushed—but—uh—I'm not coming to your party. I'm—uh—well, I'm not exactly feeling up to it.

JANET: Gee, I'm sorry, Eileen.

EILEEN: I guess I'll do our Bio homework and let you borrow it.

JANET: Why don't you try to come?

EILEEN: No—no, not tonight. [*Enthusiastically*] You ought to see the frog I cut up awhile ago. It's a beauty! I'll bring it over tomorrow. Uh—if I'm feeling better. I'll label the parts and let you keep them.

JANET: [*Weakly*] That's awfully kind of you.

EILEEN: [*Dolefully*] Good-by, Jan. Have fun.

A Party Is Born • **225**

JANET: We'll miss you. [*Phones black out. Reentering living room from R.*] Ira, who do you suppose isn't coming? Eileen!

IRA: Still scared of boys, eh?

RED: That quiz kid'll never grow up.

IRA: One less wallflower, anyway.

DAD: Janet, we've got everything planned. Now everyone take heed. Red, you lift this end of the piano. . . .

RED: [*Saluting smartly*] Righto.

DAD: And Ira, you tackle that one.

IRA: Okay, Dad.

DAD: Honey, you and I'll pull out the rug. Get over near Ira. With a little cooperation we'll have this job done. [RED *takes hold of one edge of the piano,* DAD *near him.* IRA *grips the other end,* JANET *nearby.*] Janet, squat way down. Like me. [JANET *obeys. Cumbersomely shifting to knees*] Phew! I'm nobody's spring chicken!

RED: Been breaking training, eh, Mr. Lossing?

DAD: You said it. Don't I look it? Everybody ready?

RED: All set.

IRA: Yup.

DAD: Okay, here 'tis.One, two, three—hip! [IRA *and* RED *raise the piano.* DAD *and* JANET *tug at the rug and manage to pull it clear. Snorting with satisfaction,* DAD *starts rising and loses his balance.*] Ooops, my knees! [*Collides with* RED *who valiantly clings to the piano. It plunks softly against the wall.*]

RED: [*Lowering piano with* IRA] Yikes!

IRA: Nice work, gang.

RED: That was a close call.

DAD: [*Brushing trousers*] Sorry about the collision, Red. Clumsy of me. Well, kiddies, wasn't so tough with your ol' Daddy at the helm, was it?

JANET: Nobly done, Dad.

IRA: C'mon, Red, let's stow the rug away. [IRA *and* RED *roll up the rug.* JANET *happily executes several dance turns. Suddenly she spies the wall behind piano.*]

JANET: [*Appalled*] Look at the wall! Look at the dent!

IRA: [*Stopping work*] Oh-oh! Some scar!

DAD: Wow! [*Crosses, fingers damage ruefully.*] Say, I made a nick, didn't I?

RED: [*Right behind him*] Good grief, did we do that?

DAD: There you have it, children. You can't beat it. Crime will out.

IRA: [*Singsonging*] Mom's gonna know! Bet she spots it right away.

JANET: [*Distraughtly*] Sure! And I told her everything was fine! Oh, Daddy, everything's worse'n ever. I'm sorry I got you all into this! I could call the whole party off right now!

DAD: Whoa—whoa there, honey! Let's face the problem. We're adults. It'll cost me a lot to fix that wall, but I'm not moaning and groaning about it. Not yet, I'm not! Now how can we postpone the hour of reckoning? Eh?

RED: If you're going to show movies, we could hang the screen there.

IRA: If we had a dog we could post a sign there, "Beware of Dog." Or how about "Don't Feed the Goldfish"?

JANET: [*Dolefully*] I wish I felt like joking.

DAD: [*Inspired*] I have it, honey! [*Takes portrait from mantel and sets it down strategically on piano.*] How about it? The picture hides the scar, doesn't it? [*All back off to consider.*]

RED: That ought to do the trick, Mr. Lossing. In my house we'd get away with it.

DAD: [*Wryly*] Is your mom an eagle-eye like my wife?

RED: She's no slouch.

DAD: Maybe we'll get by till morning.

JANET: [*Impetuously, embracing him*] Oh, Daddy, you're wonderful! I absolutely adore you! [*Phone D.R. rings and is illuminated. Resignedly*] It's for me. [*Runs off R.*]

IRA: Red, let's get this culprit out of the way.

RED: Sure thing. [JANET *appears at phone D.R. Light comes up on phone D.L., disclosing* PAUL CROWLEY. *He is sedate, in his late teens.* IRA *and* RED *finish rolling the rug and cart it off L.,* DAD *following.*]

JANET: [*Into phone*] Hello.

PAUL: This is Paul Crowley. May I speak to Janet, please.

JANET: Here I am, Paul.

PAUL: Oh, hello. I'm—uh—over at church. Happy birthday.

JANET: Thank you, Paul.

PAUL: To come right to the point . . . I have some bad news. The Exec. Council of the League's holding an emergency meeting tonight.

JANET: [*Disappointedly*] Oh, my!

PAUL: Looks like a long session. The four of us you're expecting'll duck out soon as we can. I promise. But it may be late—around eleven.

JANET: [*Dismayed*] That *is* late!

PAUL: I'm awfully sorry. But you see. . . .

JANET: [*Remembering manners*] I understand, Paul. Thanks loads for letting me know.

PAUL: Save a dance for me. Good-by, Janet.

JANET: Good-by. [*Phone D.L. blacks out.*] Oh, Christopher! [*Phone D.R. blacks out.*]

IRA: [*Reentering living room from L.*] Well, that's it, ol' boy.

RED: [*Reentering*] Whenever you want housewrecking done, call on me.

IRA: Wasn't your fault, feller. Bring your wire recorder later. [JANET *enters R.*]

RED: Sure. So long, Jan. See you anon.

JANET: Thanks for helping, Red. [RED exits R. JANET starts returning trappings to piano. *Abashedly*] Ira, I've been wondering—do you think you could dig up some extra boys?

IRA: Who backed out now? What celebrities aren't coming?

JANET: Oh, no one backed out! The fellows in the League have a meeting and they'll—er—be a little late.

IRA: [*Sympathetically*] Tch. You're getting all the breaks! Well, I'll see who I can round up. But no guarantees.

JANET: You're a honey.

IRA: Save the soft-soap. And now, slave driver, if you can spare my services, I'll shower. [*Front doorbell rings.*]

JANET: [*Tensely*] Guess that's Mom!

DAD: [*Blithely, entering L.*] The doorbell—I heard the doorbell, Janet. [*Retrieving punch and newspaper*] Could be your first guest! I'll duck. [*Exiting L.*] Guidebooks for parents say, "Don't hang around!"

JANET: [*Flustered*] Ira, you answer. Please—will you?

IRA: Not me. My bahth awaits. [*Exits L. Doorbell rings again. JANET exits R.*]

MOM: [*Off*] Hello, darling. Any company come yet?

JANET: [*Off*] No, Mom.

MOM: [*Off*] Take these, Jan. [*JANET comes on carrying parcels. Following*] I thought that bus'd never get here! Pokey and crowded!

JANET: [*Setting parcels on end table*] What'd you bring?

MOM: Grandma's silver tea service. Janney, honey, you look excited! What's been going on?

JANET: [*Quaveringly*] Nothing.

MOM: Nothing?

JANET: Not . . . very much, Mom. I—I just need lipstick.

MOM: [*Lightly*] Didn't you plan to be the languid hostess? Like Yvonne?

JANET: Well, you see, Mom—um—[IRA *appears in doorway L., shirt over arm.*] I started to—well, you see Red came over and—er—and. . . . [*Impulsively*] Gee, Mom, I ought to tell you something. I'd better con—confess.

IRA: [*Entering L.*] Hey, you can't turn stool-pigeon now! What was the point of all that. . . . ?

JANET: [*Tearfully*] I was cracked!

IRA: You're a big baby! You make me break my back. . . .

JANET: You didn't *have* to.

IRA: That's what you say *now!*

JANET: You—you eavesdropper! You get me so mad I . . . could. . . .

MOM: That's enough, children! Ira, put those in the kitchen. And get ready for the party.

IRA: [*Scoops up parcels. Grumbling, exiting L.*] Girls, girls! Why were they ever invented?

MOM: Now, Janet, this—er—ah—confession. Is it going to put me in a bad mood?

JANET: Yes, Mom. I'm afraid it will.

MOM: Oh. That's not so good. [*Stalling*] The room looks lovely this way, Jan—though I still think you ought to 've consulted me about the rug.

JANET: Well, Mom, I was. . . .

MOM: Isn't it a bit . . . arty to leave your picture way back there? Did you try it on the mantel?

JANET: [*Gulping*] Yes, Mom, I did.

MOM: I'd like to see how it looks. [*Starts U.L.*]

JANET: [*Beseechingly*] Let's not fool with it now, Mom! [DAD *appears in doorway L.*]

MOM: There'll be so many people here. I think it'll be safer. . . .

DAD: Hi, Betty.

MOM: Oh, hello, Walt. When'd you get back?

DAD: Awhile ago, honey. [*Hustles to* MOM'*s side. Just as* MOM *reaches for picture, he slips an arm around her shoulder and leads her C*.] Grandma feeling better? How's my favorite mom-in-law?

MOM: She's fairly comfortable, dear.

JANET: [*Stanchly*] Look, Mom, what I wanted to tell you. . . .

MOM: Dad, Janney has some sort of confession.

DAD: Is that right?

JANET: [*Doggedly, head bowed*] I'd like to—to get it off my chest. [DAD *clears throat and waves* MOM *a signal to cut* JANET *short.* MOM *nods*.] You see, Mom, when you phoned from Grandma's. . . .

MOM: Janet, babe, if it's important let's save it for tomorrow. I'd rather not have a fuss tonight.

JANET: Thing is, Mom, it seems. . . .

MOM: Just pretend you've told me. So you'll feel good too!

DAD: [*Booming*] Very sensible!

JANET: [*Puzzled*] But Mom, are you sure . . . ?

MOM: Well, we mustn't let anything spoil the party. We want it to be really special. Isn't that what we've both worked so hard for?

JANET: [*Reverently*] Gee, Mom, you're terrific! Honest!

DAD: It's what we've all worked hard for! This party'd better be good. And noisy. I like *noisy* parties! [*Phone D.R. rings and is illuminated.*] But not telephones! That must be for you, honey. [JANET *exits R.*]

MOM: Now what is this all about?

DAD: [*Finger to lips*] Shh! [*Leads* MOM *U.L. to piano.* JANET *appears at phone D.R.*]

JANET: [*Into phone*] Hello. Yes, Operator, I'll hold on. [DAD *raises portrait, revealing scar.*]

MOM: [*Gasping*] Walter Lossing! [DAD *hurriedly replaces portrait, pokes fingers in ears, and scurries off L.* MOM *follows in pursuit of explanation. Light comes up on phone D.L., disclosing* DAVEY JENNINGS. *He is smooth, ingratiating, in his late teens.*]

DAVEY: [*Into phone*] Hello?

JANET: Hello.

DAVEY: [*Giving out*] Hello, Janet. This is your newest and stanchest admirer!

JANET: [*Cooing*] Oh—Davey!

DAVEY: I'm glad you got that one right! Say, give ear, dream boat. I've got a real favor to ask!

JANET: What is it, Davey?

DAVEY: Well, about eight of my classmates are at my house now. You've heard, haven't you, that I go to the State U.?

JANET: I—I've heard.

DAVEY: I've been telling the boys what a smooth number you are —and they'd kind of like to come along tonight.

JANET: Oh, really?

DAVEY: They're a swell bunch. Strong dancers and weak appetites! What do you say, buttercup?

JANET: [*Controlling intense pleasure*] Why, Davey, I'm sure it would be perfectly all right. I'd be happy to have them.

DAVEY: [*Calling off*] Ahoy thar, brethren, the welcome mat is down! [*Into phone. Giving his all*] Thanks, Jan. See you later, stupendous!

JANET: [*Purring*] Good-by, Davey. [*Phone D.L. blacks out. JANET hangs up slowly, sighing beatifically. Phone D.R. blacks out. JANET pirouettes into the living room from R. IRA enters L. draped in a bath sheet.*]

IRA: Trouble, trouble! I heard the phone ring. Who do you want me to invite now? Kindergarten crowd? Or the punchball team?

JANET: [*Airily*] None of your corn, Ira Lossing! *That* was Davey Jennings!

IRA: Oh—the fellow who likes potato salad!

JANET: Well, he's bringing eight classmates to help him eat it! Can you imagine? Eight, Ira! The party'll be sensational! Yippeee! [*Hugs IRA and waltzes him around merrily. Phone and doorbells all ring.*]

The Curtain Falls.

NOTES ON STAGING

A PARTY Is Born takes the hurdles just before a sweet-sixteen celebration. There is much fun as familiar characters run this "obstacle course."

Production-wise, the play has some pretty special assets:

The simple set unfolds action in different places at once. (This device can safely be labeled "intriguing.") Five of the roles, though "character" bits, fit tyros as well as seasoned actors. Seen only at a telephone, the players are free of those bugaboos: walking, standing still, doing *something* with hands. If time is tight, these roles can be rehearsed separately.

Acting

Mainstay JANET is on stage nearly all the play. She acts opposite parents, brother, aunt, and assorted friends, zipping through peaks and valleys of emotion. Yep, the part is a plum.

Reminders: each phone and doorbell ring should seem to catch JAN unawares. And she and her callers should never let on if they can see each other across stage.

IRA is older than JAN, tolerant, helpful, and quick with brotherly banter.

MOM LOSSING is young in spirit, gracious, and poised. Up on psychology trends, she tries to be understanding. But she is no easy mark.

DAD thinks well of himself, his wife, his children. He is jovial, a little pompous, no longer spry.

In shouting off stage, RED should be audible. On stage he is sincere and affable.

About the five telephone bits: AUNT HELEN never suspects she is a bore. Posturing show-off YVONNE might perch on the table while speaking. EILEEN is timid about boys and parties—though not about dissection! PAUL is sedate and correct. DAVEY, man of the hour, is sure he has a way with women. He might prop a foot irreverently on the chair.

Of course there is chance for great individuality in the position of JAN'S callers (MOM included). The director can work out different ways for them to face, stand, sit. Really, the actors, rather than the scenery, set the stage in the phone nook down left.

Scenery and Furnishings

The LOSSING living room is the main set. Use flats, drapes and/or screens (see Guide) for it. Leave space near the footlights for two small areas down right and down left. They are your telephone nooks. More on them anon.

The doors and window need not "work," can stay open throughout. Substitute an archway for the door at right if you like.

The fireplace up center is merely decorative. Use a "fireplace flat" (see Guide), improvise, or substitute a table, desk, bookcase, etc.

The piano (rather bulky) and rug (a good size and wedged under it) are indispensable. Most theaters have pianos. Borrow a rug from a home, second-hand dealer.

Add festive touches to the room—streamers, balloons, flowers —what you will. It is being cleared for dancing, so may convincingly be somewhat underfurnished.

Backing for the door at right may suggest a section of hall. An end table with bric-a-brac can stand before it. JANET exits through this door to answer her phone.

Set up backing (flat, drape, or screen) for the area down right designated the "LOSSING telephone nook" (see Ground Plan). It can be non-attention-arresting. Lighting should direct audience eyes to the only furnishings required: a table, chair, and phone. Add adornment if you wish.

Keep backing and furnishings—no more than a table, chair, and phone—nondistinctive in the nook down left. It is lit for each of JAN's six callers with no change of scenery.

The routes actors take to approach the telephones depend on convenience. They can come in through overlap openings in the backings—or around the sides of drapes if they are used. Or they can simply slip in between the downstage edges of the set and the theater's tormentors.

Wondering why JAN does not step straight from the living room to the nook? Going out the door emphasizes that her phone is in another room and that it is bothersome to keep answering it.

Properties

Borrow the phones from the telephone company. Usually advance notice is needed.

If there is no portrait of your JANET, enlarge a snapshot or borrow one. A poor likeness will not be spotted across the footlights.

Know a florist or gardener who will donate real flowers? Otherwise use artificial ones for the corsage. They will stay "fresh"!

Costumes and Make-up

JAN'S formal gown strikes a gala note. Do not let the few wisps of hair still in pincurls keep her from looking lovely.

MOM is well-groomed. Omit a hat and coat when she comes home, for it can be assumed she deposits them in a hall closet. See the Guide about middle-age make-up for MOM and DAD.

DAD wears a suit. IRA dresses very informally, appearing in a bath sheet at the finale.

RED, his dressing interrupted, has slipped on moccasins and a sweater with good trousers. If the actor is not a carrot top, tint his hair with copper dust or a rinse. Or see that the name is changed to "Ted"!

AUNT HELEN'S garb is dowdy (probably a housedress), her appearance plain. YVONNE'S dressing gown can be a "creation," her face smeared with beauty cream, her hair tied back. EILEEN is bespectacled, mousy in everyday clothes.

PAUL'S suit is conservative. DAVEY flashes in a stylish jacket and brilliant tie.

Special Effects and Lighting

Bells, bells, bells—they sound off in this show. Recommended are a chime for the front door, a buzzer for the back, a record for the phone. The Special-effects section of the Guide tells about them and alternatives. *Caution:* rehearse cues! Nix on jingles when there should be jangles!

A few possibilities for the "dent" the piano nudges in the wall: (a) Put the scar on *before* the performance and count on the audience's not noticing till JAN points it out. It is upstage out of plain view. Or else—(b) make or paint the gash beforehand, pin or tape a cover over it, and have RED slip it off during the melee. Your covering should match the wall; the dent should be an obvious off-color. Or else—(c) have RED doctor the wall with a broad crayon or chalk while at the piano. Or—(d) make the dent from backstage during the scuffle by pinching in a drape, yanking a string hitched to a covering, puncturing a flat, etc.

By the bye, the play has been done with the dent left imaginary. Works, too. A place blocked by the piano was pointed at.

Lights for *A Party Is Born* aid in putting over the novel staging. No complicated system is needed, just attention to cues.

Set your lights (see Guide for particulars) for the living room. Then arrange independent illumination—spotlight (preferable) or flood—for the two phone nooks. Focus on the people, not their surroundings.

How is your equipment? You might like to vary the color of the light thrown on the nook down left to suggest change of scene and mood. And you may want to dim the lights (subtly) in the living room while JAN is at the phone.

But the only changes the script *requires* are bringing up and dousing lights on the nooks. You will get credit for a most effective job if you do that neatly.

Publicity

Let the word "party" keynote a jaunty campaign. Play up the behind-the-scenes angles. This comedy pleases a wide audience—party-throwers, party-goers, party-knowers. Bring 'em in!

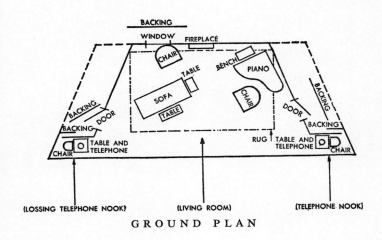

GROUND PLAN

FURNISHINGS	PROPERTIES	
sofa	vase	gift card
piano	photo album	corsage
rug	candy dishes	pin
fireplace with mantel	candy	two nickels
chairs	sheet music	telegram
end tables	bric-a-brac	filled paper bags
lamps	two telephones	glass of punch
two telephone tables	JANET'S framed	newspaper
two telephone chairs	portrait	parcels
	florist's box	

Glossary

above. Upstage of, as in a director's request, "Cross above the sofa."

ad-lib, to. To improvise words or business not in a script.

apron. Small portion of a stage extending toward the audience beyond the proscenium opening and front curtain.

baby spot. Small spotlight with intensity under 500 watts.

backdrop. Backing that rolls or slides up and down. Sometimes called a "drop."

backing. Scenery behind an opening in a set that hides off-stage area from an audience.

backstage. Stage area behind the scenery.

below. Downstage of, as in a director's request, "Cross below the sofa."

blackout. Dousing of all stage lights.

borderlight or *border.* Striplight hung over the stage in a row parallel to the footlights.

brace cleat. Metal plate with a hole to accommodate a stage brace. The cleat is screwed to the back of a flat's frame.

business. Meaningful movements and pantomime used by actors.

cast. The actors in a show.

clout nail. A short, wedge-shaped nail with a flat head used to fasten keystones and corner blocks to the joints of a flat.

corner block. Small triangular-shaped piece of three-ply veneer board used to reinforce a corner joint on a flat.

cover, to. To block a fellow actor from the sight of the audience.

crash bag. Closed sack holding fragments of glass, tin, rocks, etc. Creates crashlike noise when dropped off stage.

crepe hair. Artificial hair that comes as a braided rope. Used in making mustaches, beards, etc.

cue. Phrase or bit of action that signals an actor to speak or move. Also, one that signals a backstage worker to produce an effect.

curtain call. Appearance of a cast in response to applause when a play is over.

cyclorama or *cyc.* Curtain, canvas, or wall skirting the acting area. Generally semicircular, it is high and broad enough to mask backstage.

denouement. The final disentangling of the plot of a play.

dimmer. Electrical device for controlling the intensity of lights.

downstage. The part of the stage toward the footlights and audience. (See diagram under *stage positions.*)

drape scenery. Set of curtains used to define the acting area. Sometimes called "hangings."

dress rehearsal. Rehearsal with actors in make-up and costume—and scenery, furnishings, properties, and lights arranged and operated as for a performance. Also, the final rehearsal.

dressing stage. One or more actors moving to another position to balance the picture made by members of the cast on stage.

emcee. Master of ceremonies.

flat. Wood frame usually covered with muslin or canvas and painted. Flats are hinged or lashed together to make sections of scenery.

fly, to. To move scenery by means of rope or cable running from a gridiron.

floodlight or *flood.* Lighting unit with a reflector that projects a broad beam.

footlights or *foots.* Lights in a row at the front of the stage floor.

gelatin. Transparent paperlike material coming in many colors that gets set in front of a stage light to tint its beam. Cellophane is a substitute.

grease paint. Substance used as a base in stage make-up. (Lining pencils are also made of it.) It comes in many shades.

gridiron or *grid.* Framework above a stage, out of sight of an audience, that supports rigging when scenery is flown.

grommet. Metal eyelet.

ground plan. Layout of scenery and furniture on stage.

highlight. Light line used in stage make-up to accentuate wrinkles, prominences, and hollows.

house. A theater; a theater audience.

keystone. Small keystone-shaped piece of three-ply veneer board used to reinforce the joining of a toggle to a stile on a flat.

lash cleat. Metal hook over which a lash line is thrown when binding flats together. It is screwed to the back of a flat's frame.

lash line. Rope used in binding flats together.

lash-line eye. Metal eye to which the upper end of a lash line is secured. It is screwed to the back of a flat's frame, in the upper right corner.

light plot. Record of the placement, color, and intensity of lights plus cues for changing them during a play.

lines. An actor's speeches.

lining pencil or *liner.* Thin stick of grease paint used in making up.

nut. Amount of money invested in a production.

pantomime. Action without dialogue that expresses meaning.

patron. One who donates funds, service, advice, or moral support to a producing group.

portiere. A curtain hung at a doorway, either in place of a door or as decoration.

practical. Capable of being actually used. The term is applied to scenery and props: doors, windows, food, etc.

prompt book. Copy of a play showing all changes, additions, and deletions in lines and action arrived at by a director.

prompter. Person posted off stage with prompt book, ready to remind an actor in low tones of lines or movement he has forgotten.

property or *prop.* Item placed or handled on stage, exclusive of scenery and heavy furniture.

proscenium. Front wall of a stage with a large opening—often an arch —through which the audience views the acting area.

rail. Cross piece of lumber at the top or bottom of a flat's frame.

saddle iron. Strip of metal used to reinforce the bottom opening of a door, fireplace flat, etc.

set, to. To "set the stage" is to place scenery, furnishings, and props in position for a show.

set piece. Detached unit of scenery like a tree, boulder, pillar, platform, flight of steps, etc.

sides. Copy of one actor's lines, stage directions, and cues.

sight lines. Range of vision of spectators viewing the stage.

size water or *size.* Mixture of melted flake or ground glue and water used as a binder in scene paint.

spattering. Method of flicking drops of paint on scenery.

Spelvin. Surname often used in programs to avoid revealing that an actor is doubling in a role.

spirit gum. Adhesive mixture of gum arabic and ether used to attach false hair to the skin.

spotlight or *spot.* Lighting unit with a lens that throws a concentrated beam on a limited area.

stage brace. Device made of two adjustable lengths of wood that supports flat scenery.

stage directions. Matter in the text of a play on setting, lighting, movement, and intonation. It is generally put in italics to distinguish from actors' lines.

stage positions. Commonly used divisions of the stage area that simplify direction. "Down" is toward the footlights, "Up" away from them. "Left" and "Right" in most play texts mean from an *actor's* standpoint as he faces an audience. Terms are combined as in "Up Left" and "Down Right"—and are often abbreviated as in "U.L."

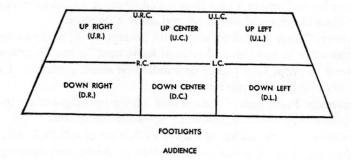

stile. Vertical piece of lumber in the frame of a flat.

strike, to. To take apart and remove a stage set.

striplight or *strip.* Row of lights in a trough, sometimes with individual reflectors.

switchboard. An apparatus that provides central control of electrical circuits.

teaser. Adjustable hanging commonly suspended just behind the proscenium to mask the top of scenery and the overhead area.

thunder sheet. Metal sheet hung backstage so it can be struck or shaken to create a sound effect.

toggle bar. Reinforcing cross piece of lumber at or near the center of a flat's frame. It parallels the rails.

tormentor. Screen on each side of the stage. It is directly behind the proscenium, masking the downstage edges of scenery and off-stage areas.

upstage. The part of the stage away from the footlights and audience. (See diagram under *stage positions.*)

wait for laughs, to. To pause artfully in acting while the audience is laughing so lines do not go unheard.

walk-on. An acting part with no lines.

wind machine. Device used backstage to imitate the sound of wind.

wing. Off-stage space to the right or left of the acting area. Also, a screen at the side of the stage parallel to the tormentor and masking off-stage areas.